Lehrerhandbuch
FOKUS DEUTSCH
Hilfe

Corinna Schicker

Sharon Brien

Sheila Brighten

Steve Williams

für **AQA**

OXFORD
UNIVERSITY PRESS

OXFORD
UNIVERSITY PRESS

Great Clarendon Street, Oxford OX2 6DP

Oxford University Press is a department of the University of Oxford.
It furthers the University's objective of excellence in research, scholarship,
and education by publishing worldwide in

Oxford New York

Athens Auckland Bangkok Bogotá Bombay Buenos Aires Cape Town
Chennai Dar es Salaam Delhi Florence Hong Kong Istanbul Karachi
Kolkata Kuala Lumpur Madrid Melbourne Mexico City Mumbai Nairobi
Paris São Paulo Shanghai Singapore Taipei Tokyo Toronto Warsaw

and associated companies in Berlin Ibadan

Oxford is a registered trademark of Oxford University Press in the UK and in
certain other countries

© Oxford University Press 2001
The moral rights of the authors have been asserted
Database right Oxford University Press
First published 2001

All rights reserved. This publication may not be reproduced, stored in a
retrieval system, or transmitted, in any forms or any means, without the prior
permission in writing of Oxford University Press, or as expressly permitted by
law, or under terms agreed with the appropriate reprographics organization.
Enquiries concerning reproduction outside the scope of the above should be
sent to the Rights Department, Oxford University Press, at the address above.

You must not circulate this book in any other binding or cover and you must
impose this same condition on any acquirer.

ISBN 0 19 912335 7

Acknowledgements

The authors and publishers would like to thank Colin Smith-Markl,
Hollingworth High School, Milnrow for his help and advice.

The recordings were produced by Lynne Brackley at The Soundhouse, London.

Typeset and designed by Steve Williams, WortSchatz Publishing Services

Printed in Great Britain by St. Edmundsbury Press Ltd., Bury St. Edmunds.

Contents

Introduction

The course	iv
Course components	iv
Teaching approach	v
Differentiation	vi
Teaching notes	1–50
Answers	51

INTRODUCTION

The course

Welcome to *Fokus Deutsch Hilfe für AQA*.

These workbooks are revised editions of the *Fokus Deutsch Hilfe* workbooks, which were produced in response to requests from teachers for materials designed specifically for Foundation Tier and borderline candidates. The new editions follow the unit sequence of the *Fokus Deutsch für AQA* course-book, and will assist in preparing students in Years 10 and 11 for Key Stage 4 of the National Curriculum. Like the main course, *Fokus Deutsch Hilfe für AQA* is particularly compatible with the new AQA specifications A and B.

Although the *Fokus Deutsch Hilfe für AQA* workbooks are intended primarily to help students preparing for the Foundation Tier of GCSE, much of the material will be suitable for use with candidates who are working towards an Entry Level Certificate (ELC).

Most of the boards' specifications contain written and spoken coursework assignments. The *Du bist dran!* pages in *Fokus Deutsch Hilfe für AQA* may be used to give such students guidance in preparing spoken coursework, and there are many suggestions for written follow-up tasks, which could form the basis for written coursework.

The aims of the workbooks are as follows:

- to build up students' confidence by providing simple, manageable tasks which can be done instead of, or as an introduction to, more challenging tasks in the main course-book
- to highlight a limited number of basic structures, and some basic vocabulary, some of which is set out in the individual tasks in the form of *Hilfe* boxes
- to provide a balanced range of listening, speaking, reading, and writing activities
- to allow scope for whole-class exercises, group tasks, pair-work, and individual research
- to maximize the use of the target language and to encourage learner autonomy
- to practise basic dictionary skills
- to provide a mixture of 'fun' items

Course components

Fokus Deutsch Hilfe für AQA consists of two workbooks (*Arbeitsheft 1* and *Arbeitsheft 2*), a teacher's book (*Lehrerhandbuch*), and a single cassette or CD, which may be duplicated to support individual study.

Die Arbeitshefte

- follow the four modules of AQA specification B (modular) and the four units of AQA specification A:
  Arbeitsheft 1 1: *Meine Welt*, 2: *Ferien und Reisen*
  Arbeitsheft 2 3: *Arbeit und Freizeit*, 4: *Junge Leute heute*
- have a clear layout, numbered activities, and a clear indication of where to use any recorded material
- contain tasks which practise the four skills, and provide for individual study, pair-work, and whole-class activities
- contain end-of-module *Kontrollen* in all four skills for assessment purposes
- provide a simple self-assessment sheet of 'I can...' statements for each module. These *Kontrollseiten* can be used by students to monitor their own progress.

Das Lehrerhandbuch

- suggests appropriate ways, and times, of using *Fokus Deutsch Hilfe für AQA* in conjunction with the main course-book
- gives detailed teaching notes, including suggestions for maximizing use of the target language
- provides full transcripts of all recorded material

Die Kassette/CD

- contains material recorded at a moderate speed, with a range of speakers/voices

INTRODUCTION

Teaching approach

No one teaching approach is prescribed in this manual, but it is hoped that teachers using the course will find the teaching suggestions useful and interesting. The tasks are as varied as possible, and include a range of games, puzzles and surveys.

The course follows closely the topics found in *Fokus Deutsch für AQA*, and is intended to provide additional material, particularly for Foundation Tier candidates. It is hoped that teachers will be able to use the workbooks in a flexible manner. It is envisaged that students will normally follow the *Fokus Deutsch für AQA* course-book, which contains vocabulary and structure guides, and then branch off into workbook activities to consolidate this work. In some instances, teachers may prefer to use activities from the workbooks as an alternative to activities in the main course-book. On the whole, the activities match GCSE-type tasks, for example matching exercises, true/false/not in text sentences, multiple-choice, simple gap-filling and so on. At the same time, they are intended to be varied and enjoyable in order to make the use of the course as a whole more effective.

The *Lehrerhandbuch* contains guidance on how the material in the workbooks can be used to support the teaching of the main course. In some instances, teachers may decide that the material in the workbooks provides a more accessible starting point for a topic area than the main course-book. For this reason, *Hilfe* boxes, containing only the essential structures required to carry out an activity, are provided where appropriate.

Encouraging student autonomy

The use of the workbooks will encourage student autonomy, giving students the opportunity to work independently on some of the activities. The development of dictionary skills is encouraged in many of the reading activities. Students could tackle some of the listening activities in small groups, while others work on reading or writing tasks. Some of the activities may be exploited further by asking students to develop their own version of the activity in a creative and imaginative way. Suggestions for such follow-up work are signalled in the detailed teaching notes.

Additionally, follow-up tasks, reading, writing and cassette-based speaking tasks can equally be considered both as homework tasks and as additional assessment tasks to supplement the *Kontrolle* sections, as well as classroom-based tasks. Students should be encouraged not to see them simply as more work but rather as a bonus for doing well, hence the use of ICT or fun-based tasks.

Reading

The reading activities in the workbooks contain a more limited amount of vocabulary and structures than those in the main course-book. Nevertheless, students should still be encouraged to use dictionaries to look up unfamiliar vocabulary. Attempts are made in many activities to broaden the range of students' vocabulary.

A possible approach to tackling reading passages with students is as follows:

- study the layout, title and visuals accompanying the text
- ask students to predict or anticipate answers to questions
- skim the text to confirm predictions
- read more closely to find all the required information

Listening

The listening material in *Fokus Deutsch Hilfe für AQA* is intended to develop students' confidence in this skill area by limiting the amount of German they hear, and by recycling language they have already met in reading exercises. The amount of reading required in the tasks is kept to a minimum, and extensive use is made of visual clues and stimuli. The number of times students listen to the recording is left to the discretion of the teacher.

Here is a possible approach to listening activities:

- encourage the students to anticipate answers (pre-listening), using visual clues, etc.
- predict certain key items of vocabulary, and write these on the board or an OHT
- confirm or revise predictions after first listening (which could simply be to listen out for the key words already identified)
- listen again, concentrating on specific relevant information

Writing

Writing activities, or suggestions for further written exploitation of material, are based mainly on students adapting models. Written work follows extensive speaking, listening and reading

INTRODUCTION

practice of key phrases and structures. Certain activities provide carefully prepared, closed answers in an attempt to reinforce structures. On the other hand, it is hoped that many of the activities will lead to the production of more open-ended pieces of writing.

Written work, display or project work can be carried out in a variety of ways, for example, written up by hand following drafting in rough; drafting in rough using ICT and then correcting using ICT. This method both motivates the less able, who might find writing legibly and neatly difficult, and encourages and stretches the more able student to produce more than the minimum required for the task by using a combination of handwritten work and ICT: for example, ICT can be used to produce visuals, where students find drawing difficult or their drawing skills are somewhat immature and these can be accompanied by handwritten text or vice versa. All artwork, charts and diagrams to accompany tasks can be produced using ICT, old magazines, photographs, etc. and should not be seen as exclusively drawing tasks. Grids and charts could be templated by more able students or the teacher onto the ICT network for all or less able students to complete.

Speaking

Students are encouraged to use the target language in a variety of contexts. There are suggestions for class surveys, pair- and group-work, question and answer exercises, as well as the *Du bist dran!* cue pages for Modules 1 and 2. Many of the listening and reading activities could form the basis of whole-class oral work, which in turn could lead to group discussion.

Using the *Du bist dran!* pages

These cue pages are intended to provide effective preparation of spoken assignments and tests. For Module 1, the *Du bist dran!* pages provide specimen questions on a given topic, together with sample and model answers, intended to give students the necessary structures and vocabulary to prepare their own replies. These pages may be used in a flexible manner. Some teachers may wish to use the model answer as an additional reading exercise, and then encourage students to use it as a model for preparing their own answers. Alternatively, teachers may wish to encourage students to recognize and answer the questions in section 1, before moving on to fuller answers. There is also opportunity for pair-work at this stage. The *Du bist dran!* pages for Module 2 follow a different format. There are two pages covering the present, future and past tenses. The cues on these pages will provide the basis for more open-ended oral work. For Modules 3 and 4, detailed cues are provided on the *Kontrolle* pages.

Differentiation

Although the material in **Fokus Deutsch Hilfe für AQA** is aimed primarily at Foundation Tier level, some of the tasks are slightly more demanding and require more extensive reading or listening practice. Many of the suggested written tasks are open-ended and therefore differentiate by outcome. Teachers will use their professional judgement to decide how much of the target language is expected from their students in spoken work. For some students, full sentences and complex structures will be expected. For others, the ability to convey messages in a comprehensible way by using short, simple sentences will be deemed sufficient.

TEIL 1

A Hallo, wie geht's?

Page 4

1 Das deutsche ABC

a This listening task consolidates **exercise 2** on **p.6** of the main course-book on the German alphabet. Students can work on it independently after completing the course-book exercise as a whole-class activity.

- Preparation: revise the alphabet with the class. Ideas include singing the alphabet to a well-known tune, or playing a game of 'Letter Bingo' or 'Hangman'.
- Students listen to the recording and spell the hidden word.
- Follow-up: more able students spell out the names of classmates, football teams, etc. and see who recognizes the names first. Less able students are given further names to spell in German, or they suggest further names to each other.

> **Transcript**
> A-U-F W-I-E-D-E-R-S-E-H-E-N.

b This follow-up task provides additional listening practice on the German alphabet, encouraging listening in detail in order to check spelling and correct any errors found.

- Advise students to follow the spelling of each word in column one of the table and decide whether it is *falsch* or *richtig* during the first playing of the recording. If they decide it is *falsch*, they can use subsequent playings to write down the correct spelling in the third column.
- Less able students may need to refer to the main course-book **p.6** to check letter sounds during the playing of the recording.
- Follow-up: the teacher or students spell out various names with deliberate errors for the class to correct. This can be made into a team game.

> **Transcript**
> 1 – Wie heißen Sie?
>   – Ich heiße Herr Neitz.
>   – Wie schreibt man das?
>   – N-E-I-T-Z.
> 2 – Und wie heißt du?
>   – Ich heiße Martina Baum. Meinen Vornamen schreibt man M-A-R-T-I-N-A, und meinen Nachnamen schreibt man B-A-U-M.
> 3 – Wie ist dein Name?
>   – Mein Name ist Verena.
>   – Verena? Wie buchstabiert man das?
>   – V-E-R-E-N-A.
> 4 – Wie heißen Sie?
>   – Mein Vorname ist Andreas und mein Nachname ist Frank.
>   – Wie buchstabiert man das?
>   – Das buchstabiert man so: A-N-D-R-E-A-S und F-R-A-N-K.
> 5 – Wie ist dein Name?
>   – Mein Vorname ist Florian.
>   – Florian, wie schreibt man das, bitte?
>   – F-L-O-R-I-A-N.

2 Filmstars!

a This oral pair-work task provides an alternative to **exercise 3b** on **p.7** of the main course-book.

- Pairs of students practise asking each other how to spell the filmstars' names. The student asking the question checks the spelling using **p.6** of the main course-book.
- Less able students may find it useful to use the main course-book to assist with spelling as well as checking answers. Alternatively, one student might spell the first name and another the family name.

b This additional pair-work task extends task 2a above.

- Students are allowed a non-directed choice of names to spell in German.
- More able students may wish to choose German nouns based on a different theme.

3 Wie geht's Herrn Schmidt?

This matching task will serve as an introduction or alternative to **exercise 4** on **p.7** of the main-course book.

- Preparation: revise expressions of positive and negative well-being orally with the whole class.
- Ensure that students recognize each expression before the task is completed.
- Check answers as a whole-class activity or ask students to check their answers in pairs.
- Follow-up: **exercise 5** on **p.7** of the main course-book, but without *weil*.

TEIL 1

Wir lernen uns besser kennen

Page 5

1 Die Zahlen

a This listening task provides revision of cardinal numbers and will serve as an introduction to **exercise 1** on **p.8** of the main-course book.

- Revise cardinal numbers 1–31.
- Less able students would benefit from the numbers being written on the board or OHT as well as being given orally.
- Play the recording as many times as required by students, pausing after each number for weaker students.
- Check answers as a whole-class activity or ask students to check their answers in pairs.
- Follow-up: number games, including bingo.
- For homework, students could create their own dot-to-dot pictures (or use one from a magazine) and write the joining-up sequence of numbers out in German.

Transcript
1 dreißig
2 fünfundneunzig
3 elf
4 siebzehn
5 einundfünfzig
6 achtundsiebzig
7 zweihundert
8 sechzig

b This simple follow-up task provides written reinforcement of cardinal numbers.

2 Wann haben sie Geburtstag?

a This listening task provides an easier alternative to **exercise 2** on **p.8** of the main course-book.

- Preparation: revise ordinal numbers 1–31 and months of the year. This could also take the form of a team game or pair-work task.
- Play the recording as many times as required by students, pausing after each number for weaker students.
- Check answers as a whole-class activity or ask students to check their answers in pairs. Check less able students' answers and explain the correct form where errors have occurred, before going on to do the follow-up task 2b.
- For homework, students could design birthday cards, perhaps using ICT.

Transcript
1 Ich habe am sechsten November Geburtstag.
2 Mein Geburtstag ist am einunddreißigsten Januar.
3 Ich habe am gleichen Tag wie mein Bruder Geburtstag – am zwölften April.
4 Ich feiere meinen Geburtstag am sechsundzwanzigsten Mai.
5 Und mein Geburtstag ist am neunten Februar.

b This simple follow-up pair-work task provides additional oral practice of stating one's birthday in German, and is based on the pictures from task 2a above.

- Follow-up: ask students to state their own birthday. Students question each other about their birthdays.
- More able students could conduct a questionnaire of the class's birthdays and present the findings orally or in written form.

c This additional follow-up task provides written reinforcement of dates with *am*.

3 Das bin ich!

This listening task will serve as an introduction to **exercise 3** on **p.8** of the main course-book. It brings together in one task the different aspects of the topic covered so far in the main course-book.

- Preparation: revise personal information orally and aurally, including giving one's name, date of birth, age, place of birth and telephone number.
- Preparation: students could practise similar language in pairs and groups, including noting down information given.
- Students listen to the recording and choose the correct answer.
- Less able students may require the recording to be played in sections, and each section to be repeated before proceeding to the next section.
- Students check their answers in pairs.
- Follow-up: additional questioning on the material:
  T: *Wie alt ist Christoph? Was ist sein Geburtsort? Buchstabiert das!* etc.
- More able students could use the task to create a written or recorded profile of themselves. This could be set as class work or for homework.

> **Transcript**
>
> Ich heiße Christoph Schmidt. Also, mein Vorname ist Christoph. Das schreibt man C-H-R-I-S-T-O-P-H. Mein Geburtstag? Mein Geburtstag ist am 12. Juni. Ja, ich bin fünfzehn Jahre alt. Ich bin in München geboren – das ist in Süddeutschland und das schreibt man M-Ü-N-C-H-E-N. Meine Telefonnummer ist einundsiebzig sechsundzwanzig fünfunddreißig.

Freunde und Familie

Page 6

The tasks on this page encourage students to write accurately about themselves and their families. These tasks will serve as an introduction or alternative to **exercise 1** on **p.10** of the main course-book.

- Preparation: revise the vocabulary and structures using the *Hilfe* box in the main course-book and stressing adjective endings.
- Preparation: pick a student and ask the others to describe him/her orally, using the vocabulary and structures from the *Hilfe* box.

1 Wie sind sie?

- Students match expressions to the appropriate visual.
- Follow-up: students could bring pictures of popstars, etc. into class and then create profiles for them, or attach appropriate descriptive labels.

2 Das ist mein Bruder!

a A simple gap-fill task.

- Preparation: revise descriptions, highlighting the position of the adjective and the need for adjective endings.
- Students fill the gaps with the relevant words from the *Hilfe* box.
- Less able students might benefit from working in pairs.

b In this additional writing task, students adapt the text from task 2a to describe a female family member/friend. The task can be set as homework

- Students may prefer to select a famous person rather than someone from their family.
- Alternatively, provide various pictures from magazines in a 'lucky dip'. Students select one picture and describe it orally to fellow students. The student speaking gains one point for his/her team for a correct detail given; the other team gains two points for noting an error in the accuracy of what is said.

Page 7

3 Was sind diese Tiere?

This writing task serves as an introduction or alternative to **exercise 3** on **p.10** of the main course-book, revising a wider range of animal/pet vocabulary.

- Preparation: present animal pictures on an OHT or the board. Students then mime animals or make animal sounds for the class to guess.
- Preparation: revise genders. You may wish to begin with *der*, *die* and *das* and remind students of their indefinite equivalents: *ein*, *eine* and *ein*.
- Preparation: revise animal vocabulary orally, stressing genders and the use of *ein*, *eine* or *ein*. This can be done as whole-class, team games or individual questioning.
- Students unscramble the letters to find the animal names and write them out with the appropriate indefinite article. Less able students may use a dictionary to complete the task. You may need to put dictionary abbreviations *m.*, *f.* and *n./nt.* on the board to help. Less able students may also find it helpful to cross out each letter once used to avoid duplicating letters.
- More able students check their answers by spelling the words aloud using the German alphabet. Alternatively, check answers as a whole-class activity using the board or an OHT.
- Follow-up: students may wish to create their own anagrams, possibly as a homework task.

4 Was für Haustiere haben sie?

This reading and matching task extends the vocabulary of task 3 above with basic descriptions of size and colour.

- Preparation: introduce unknown vocabulary orally and visually, using pictures drawn on the board:
  T: *Sind das lange oder kurze Ohren?* etc.
  Alternatively, students could check any unknown vocabulary in the dictionary.
- Students match the descriptions to the correct pictures.

TEIL 1

- Check answers as a whole-class activity:
  T: *Was hat lange Ohren? Was hast du geschrieben?* etc.
  Alternatively, the text could be written onto an OHT and cut into strips, and more able students could be asked to select a sentence from the pile of strips and link it to the correct animal.

5 *Einen, eine* oder *ein*?

This gap-filling task offers grammar reinforcement of accusative endings with *ein*, within the context of pets.

- Preparation: stress the need to identify gender correctly, reminding students of dictionary abbreviations *m.*, *f.* and *n./nt.* and their meanings.
- Students complete sentences orally in class first, using the article boxes, before writing a fair copy in their workbooks.
- Check answers as a whole-class activity, using a completed OHT. More able students could check their answers in pairs.

6 Wer hat Haustiere?

This is a group-work or pair-work oral task to consolidate work covered in tasks 3–5 above.

- Students ask each other whether they have a pet, using the example provided.
- For variety, students could conduct their survey in small groups, and groups could then compare results.
- Follow-up: students note their findings as they conduct the survey and then display their results. The less able may wish to use pictures and graphs, whilst the more able should be encouraged to accompany their displays with short written sentences.
- Follow-up: students write a few lines about their own pet, real or imaginary.

Page 8

The tasks on this page may be used as an introduction or alternative to **exercises 4–6** on **p.11** of the main course-book.

7 Wer ist wer?

- Preparation: revise job titles orally, including the feminine ending *-in*.
- Preparation: remind students of how many jobs they are looking for and that these can be listed vertically or horizontally.

- Students find the job titles in the word grid and list them with *der* or *die*.
- Check answers as a whole-class activity. More able students could check their answers in pairs.
- Follow-up: students design their own wordsearches for homework. Provide students with squared paper and encourage neatness and accuracy. Words could be in English with clues in German or vice versa, or all male or all female. The best wordsearches could be copied and used as a resource.
- Simple wordsearch programmes are also available on computer to assist the less able with their designs.

8 Was sind sie von Beruf?

This listening task will serve as an introduction to **exercise 5** on **p.11** of the main course-book and extends the vocabulary used in task 3 above.

- Preparation: revise job titles, including genders. Alternatively, this may be set as a homework task in preparation for the listening task.
- Check that students know the jobs and genders mentioned in the exercise.
- Play the recording as many times as required by students. Less able students may benefit from hearing the recording in small chunks.
- Students listen to the recording and complete the table.
- Check answers as a whole-class activity, or ask students to check their answers in pairs.
- Follow-up: you could ask additional questions of more able students:
  T: *Wer ist Programmierer? Ist Klaus' Vater Programmierer?* etc.

Transcript
1 – Hallo, Peter. Was ist dein Vater von Beruf?
 – Mein Vater ist Programmierer.
2 – Und du, Klaus? Was ist dein Vater?
 – Mein Vater ist Lehrer.
3 – Claudia, ist deine Mutter vielleicht auch Lehrerin?
 – Nein, meine Mutter ist Mechanikerin.
4 – Was ist deine Mutter von Beruf, Helga?
 – Meine Mutter ist Kellnerin.
5 – Und du, Manfred. Was ist dein Vater?
 – Mein Vater ist Polizist.

9 Wie ist deine Familie?

This writing exercise provides further practice of personality adjectives and nouns for family members. It will serve as an introduction or easier alternative to **exercise 7** on **p.11** of the main course-book.

- Preparation: revise personality adjectives
- Students write simple sentences about members of their family using the adjectives provided.
- Alternatively, students may prefer to write about a fictional family, e.g. a family from a soap opera.

Du bist dran!

Page 9

The tasks on this page provide basic revision of topics covered so far in **Teil 1** of the main course-book.

1 Fragen und Antworten

This task introduces students to questions and answers by means of a matching exercise. This will then provide model answers for task 3 below.

2 Mach mit!

This reading exercise involves spotting mistakes in an account similar to the answers in task 1 above.

- It may be helpful to point out to less able students the number of mistakes to be found.
- For homework, students could write about themselves in a similar way. More able students could write a correct version and then a second version on paper which includes some deliberate mistakes for their partner to read and identify the errors. They could then use the correct version or their knowledge of their fellow student to check the errors spotted.
- Alternatively, students exchange descriptions and correct one another's versions by trying to spot grammatical or spelling errors.

3 Jetzt bist du dran!

Students prepare and record their own model answers along similar lines to task 1 above, using **p.11** of the main course-book for reference. More able students should try to create a continuous account, whilst less able students could work in pairs with one person asking the questions and the other responding; they then swap roles.

B Meine Interessen

Page 10

1 Interessen

This matching task revises some basic vocabulary on the topic of leisure and interests. It will serve as an introduction to **exercise 1** on **p.12** of the main course-book.

- Preparation: revise the vocabulary and structures relating to leisure activities using the sentences provided underneath the visuals.
- Preparation: use an OHT or visuals of the interests mentioned to check comprehension orally.
- Students read sentences and link up pictures, working in pairs and/or using dictionaries if necessary.
- Students suggest answers orally in a whole-class session. They then copy out the correct answers.
- Follow-up: students could create their own list of hobbies for themselves or members of their family.
- Students could use ICT to create a display of icons with the appropriate labelling underneath. Alternatively, this could be a homework task, with students using pictures from magazines, newspapers or TV guides for the same purpose.

2 Hobbys

This listening task provides a revision of leisure activities and serves as an introduction, or alternative, to **exercise 1** on **p.12** of the main course-book.

- Students listen to the recording and identify the correct activities.
- Students listen to the recording again and identify whether the four speakers like or dislike the various hobbies.
- Check answers as a whole-class activity. Alternatively, students can check their answers in pairs.
- Follow-up: ask questions to test students' recall or ask their own preferences.
- The follow-up work suggested for task 1 above is equally relevant here.
- The less able could also use pictures of hobbies for a game of bingo.

TEIL 1

> **Transcript**
>
> 1 – Hallo, Irena. Ich mache eine Umfrage. Was sind deine Hobbys?
> – Meine Hobbys? Hmm … ich höre gern Musik und ich tanze sehr gern.
> – Und was machst du nicht gern?
> – Ich spiele nicht gern Fußball. Das finde ich langweilig und Lesen mag ich auch nicht.
> 2 – Und du, Joachim? Was machst du gern und was machst du nicht gern?
> – Ich sammle sehr gern Briefmarken und ich mag auch gern Tiere, aber ich höre nicht gern Musik. Musik finde ich zu laut!
> 3 – Helga, magst du Musik auch nicht?
> – Nein, ich höre sehr gern Musik und ich gehe auch sehr oft tanzen. Ich spiele auch gern Fußball. Briefmarkensammeln finde ich aber langweilig.
> 4 – Manfred, was sind deine Hobbys?
> – Das ist sehr einfach. Fußball mag ich nicht. Ich bin zu faul. Ich mag auch Tiere nicht. Ich lese gern den ganzen Tag in meinem Schlafzimmer – je mehr Bücher, desto besser!

Du bist dran!

Page 11

The tasks on this page provide basic revision of the topic of leisure activities from **Teil 1** of the main course-book.

1 Fragen und Antworten

This task introduces students to questions and answers by means of a matching exercise. This will then provide model answers for task 3 below.

2 Mach mit!

This written task provides an introduction or more structured alternative to **exercise 4** on **p.17** of the main course-book. The highly structured approach alleviates potential word order problems.

- Students create sentences using the three boxes listing first-person verb forms, frequency and the activity.
- More able students may be encouraged to create sentences of their own, using this task as a model.
- Less able students will require assistance to ensure that the sentences created are logical.

3 Jetzt bist du dran!

Students speak about their interests and make a cassette in a similar way. More able students should try to create a continuous account, whilst less able students could work in pairs with one person asking the questions and the other responding; they then swap roles.

Gehen wir aus?

Page 12

1 Mr Stevens geht gern aus!

a This text matching task provides students with a realistic context for the topic of buying concert tickets. Students act as 'translators' for their teacher who doesn't speak German.

- Students match German and English sentences.
- Follow-up: students can design similar English/German sentence pairs themselves in preparation for task 1b.

b This pair-work task offers oral consolidation of the phrases from task 1a.

- Students make up their own dialogues based on the cues provided.

c This follow-up written gap-fill task is an easier alternative to **exercise 6** on **p.15** of the main course-book.

- Check comprehension orally.
- Students write out the letter in full.
- This exercise could be completed on computer, to enable students to produce their own adapted versions for homework or in class.

Letztes Wochenende

Page 13

1 Gegenwart oder Vergangenheit?

This task encourages students to identify the tense of the verb, using the main course-book to help them. It serves as an introduction or alternative to **exercise 1** on **p.16** of the main course-book.

- Preparation: revise the present and perfect tenses orally.

- Students decide whether each sentence is in the past or present tense and insert the appropriate letter in the box.
- Invite students to read out their answers and explain how they made their decisions.
- Students then copy out the correct answers.
- Follow-up work: students rewrite present-tense sentences in the perfect tense and vice versa. this could either be a classwork or homework task.

2 Worträtsel

This reordering task helps students to develop a sense of correct word order when using the perfect tense.

- Preparation: revise perfect tense word order orally.
- Students rearrange the words to make meaningful sentences. They jot down their answers in rough.
- Invite students to read out their answers.
- Students copy out the correct answers.
- Follow-up task: students work in pairs. Each partner writes and then jumbles up a set of sentences to make a similar task for his/her partner to do.
- Less able students could identify sentences using the perfect tense in the main course-book and jumble those for their partner. The course-book then provides the correct sentences for students to check their work against.

3 Was fehlt?

This gap-fill task provides students with the opportunity to practise the use of *sein* and *haben* in the perfect tense. It serves as an introduction or alternative to **exercise 2b** on **p.16** of the main course-book. Students may require considerable explanation and additional practice to grasp this difficult concept.

- Preparation: revise the use of *sein* and *haben* orally.
- Students complete the sentences using the correct form of *sein* or *haben*, using the *Hilfe* box. They jot down their answers in rough.
- Invite students to read out their answers.
- Students copy out the correct sentences in full.
- Follow-up: students select from the main course-book a further five examples of sentences using *sein* and/or five using *haben* and copy them out minus the forms of *sein* or *haben* for their partner to complete. The original sentences in the main course-book provide accurate sentences for students to check their answers against.

Page 14

4 Pauls Samstag

a This ordering task is an introduction or alternative to **exercise 3** on **p.17** of the main course-book. It serves to reinforce work done earlier on daily routine in the present tense.

- Students match the sentences in the past tense to the visuals. They jot down a possible sequence in rough.
- Invite students to read out their answers
- Students copy out the full sentences in the correct sequence.
- Follow-up work: more able students could rewrite the sentences using the present tense.
- Less able students could undertake matching tasks using scrambled groups of pictures and sentences.

b This task provides a structured approach to creating a written piece of work on daily routine using the perfect tense. It also consolidates work on time and word order.

- Preparation: you may wish to break the task down into two stages: time phrases and the perfect tense. Less able students may require further revision of time, and all students will need reminding about word order.
- Students write sentences in the past tense to accompany each picture. They jot down their answers in rough first.
- Invite students to read out their answers.
- Students copy out their own answers correctly.
- Less able students may require a *Hilfe* list of possible times and possible sentences in the perfect tense from which to select. This could be provided on a worksheet, on an OHT or in a file on computer.
- More able students could use this task as a model from which to create their own strip cartoon or diary, which could be produced as classwork or homework. ICT or pictures from magazines could also be used.

TEIL 1

Du bist dran!

Page 15

The tasks on this page provide basic revision of the perfect tense, linked to activities covered in **Teil 1** of the main course-book.

1 Fragen und Antworten

This task introduces the students to questions and answers by means of a matching exercise. This will then provide model answers for task 3 below.

2 Mach mit!

This reading exercise provides a more structured introduction or alternative, to **exercise 4** on **p.17** of the main course-book.

- Students sequence the visuals to match the description in the letter.

3 Jetzt bist du dran!

Students speak about their interests and activities using the perfect tense and make a cassette. More able students should try to create a continuous account, whilst less able students could work in pairs with one person asking the questions and the other responding; they then swap roles.

C Meine Umgebung

Page 16

1 Wo liegt das?

a This matching task serves as an introduction or alternative to **exercise 1** on **p.18** of the main course-book.

- Preparation: revise location phrases orally by naming other towns on a map of the UK:
  T: *Watford – liegt das in Nordengland oder in Südengland?* etc.
- Students select the correct sentence halves to form statements about the towns on the map and their locations.
- Invite students to read out their answers.
- Students write out the correct answers in full.
- More able students could write a further set of sentences for towns of their own choice.

b This pair-work task provides oral reinforcement of task 1a above and offers an alternative to **exercise 2** on **p.18** of the main course-book. It can be done either before or after task 1a above.

2 Wo wohnst du?

This writing task serves as an introduction or an easier alternative to **exercise 5** on **p.19** of the main course-book.

- Preparation: revise the key house types/location phrases from exercises 3 and 4 on pp. 18–19 of the main course-book: *das Einfamilienhaus, die Wohnung, das Reihenhaus; an der Küste, in einer Großstadt, auf dem Land,* using sketches on the board or visuals on an OHT.
- Less able students should be provided with the key vocabulary in a *Hilfe* list, or with sentence halves to match up.
- Students write sentences to match the pictures. They jot down their answers in rough first.
- Invite students to read out their answers.
- Students write out a fair copy of their answers.

Zu Hause

Page 17

The tasks on this page provide additional practice of vocabulary and structures relating to the house from **p.20** of the main course-book.

1 Mein Haus

a This task serves as an introduction to **exercise 1** on **p.20** of the main course-book.

- Preparation: revise house vocabulary orally, stressing genders.
- Students work alone or in pairs, identifying and labelling the rooms in the house.
- Check answers as a whole-class activity, or ask students to check their own answers in pairs.

b Students consolidate the vocabulary by drawing a labelled plan, real or imaginary, of their own house.

2 Christian beschreibt sein Haus

This task provides a slightly different slant on the topic and may be used in conjunction with or as an alternative to **exercise 2** and **exercise 3** on **p.20** of the main course-book.

a This is a true/false reading task.

- Preparation: revise key room vocabulary.

- Students read Christian's description of his house and then decide whether the statements are true or false.
- Check answers as a whole-class activity.
- Follow-up: go over unknown vocabulary with the class.

b This is a simple writing task.

- Students correct the false statements.
- Follow-up: more able students may attempt to write their own description of their house and where they live, using this task as a model answer.

Page 18

3 In meinem Zimmer

This task provides some basic revision of bedroom furniture, as well as reinforcing the need for accuracy of spelling. It serves as an introduction or alternative to **exercise 4** on **p.21** of the main course-book.

- Preparation: revise furniture vocabulary orally: T: *Was ist „lamp" auf Deutsch? Was ist „das Bett" auf Englisch?* etc.
- Preparation: check that students understand the artwork.
- Students write out the nouns with *der*, *die* or *das*.
- Check answers as a whole-class activity.
- Follow-up: students create crosswords using symbols or English/German clues, or design wordsearches on the topic of furniture. Provide students with squared paper and encourage neatness and accuracy. The best crosswords/wordsearches could be copied and used as a resource.

4 Wo ist die Katze?

This light-hearted matching task provides a simpler version of **exercise 6** on **p.21** of the main course-book.

- Preparation: check comprehension of prepositions and revise their use. Students could be invited to draw simple drawings on the OHT or board and then describe them. Alternatively, they could describe objects in the room.
- Students match the sentences to the visuals.
- Check answers as a whole-class activity.
- Students make a fair copy of their answers.
- Follow-up: students could create and label their own version of *Wo ist die Katze?*, preferably using ICT.

Page 19

5 Mein Schlafzimmer: Präpositionen + Dativ

This grammar task reinforces **exercise 6** on **p.21** of the main course-book, again practising dative prepositions but in a different context.

- Working individually or in pairs, students select the correct preposition for the ten sentences describing the room illustrated.

6 Was für ein Zimmer!

This grammar task follows on from task 5 above by building on the use of dative prepositions to describe the contents of a room, whilst requiring greater creativity from the students themselves.

- Using the *Hilfe* box provided, students make up their own descriptions of this mixed-up room, following the example given.
- Less able students will require additional support, whilst more able students should enjoy the opportunity for free practice of the language acquired.

Meine Meinung

Page 20

1 Was gibt es in der Stadt?

a This reordering task will serve as an introduction or alternative to **exercise 1** on **p.22** of the main course-book.

- Preparation: revise the necessary town vocabulary with the class, e.g. write key nouns (*die Eisbahn, das Theater, das Stadion*, etc.) on the board or an OHT, and then mime the associated activity, while students select the relevant noun from the list. This could take the form of a team game, with the student who guesses correctly taking the next turn to mime.
- Preparation: revise genders. You may wish to begin with *der*, *die* and *das* and remind students of their indefinite equivalents: *ein*, *eine* and *ein*.
- Students unscramble the letters to find the place names and write them out with the appropriate indefinite article.
- Less able students may use a dictionary to complete the task. Put dictionary abbreviations *m.*, *f.* and *n./nt.* on the board to help. Less able students may also find it helpful to cross out

TEIL 1

each letter once used to avoid duplicating letters.
- More able students check their answers by spelling the words aloud using the German alphabet. Otherwise, check answers as a whole-class activity.

b This listening task will serve as an introduction or alternative to **exercise 1** on **p.22** of the main course-book and helps to consolidate the vocabulary in task 1a above.

- Preparation: revise *es gibt einen/eine/ein* and *keinen/keine/kein*, also *(nicht) viele*.
- Students hear four descriptions of cities. They indicate in the table which buildings are in which city.
- Check answers as a whole-class activity.
- Follow-up: students prepare their own description of their town or a town of their choice, real or imaginary. This could be undertaken in class or as a homework task.
- Less able students could prepare a poster using material from the local authority website, local newspaper or travel brochures, selecting pictures and labelling them correctly.
- More able students could use the same sources to produce a town brochure with a sentence about each building.

Transcript
1 Salzburg ist eine alte Stadt in Österreich. Sie hat ein altes Theater und auch viele Restaurants. Es gibt aber kein Sportzentrum in der Stadtmitte.
2 Köln ist eine alte Stadt in Deutschland. Es gibt viele Restaurants in der Stadtmitte und auch ein Theater. Köln hat ein Stadion und es gibt auch ein schönes Sportzentrum.
3 Wien ist die Hauptstadt von Österreich. Sie hat ein sehr altes Theater und ein modernes Stadion. Wien hat nicht viele Jugendklubs, aber es gibt ein großes Sportzentrum.
4 München ist eine moderne Stadt. Es gibt viel zu tun und zu sehen. Das Sportzentrum ist ausgezeichnet und das Stadion ist auch sehr neu.

2 Die Stadt hat …

This non-directed writing task extends the town vocabulary from task 1 and will serve as an introduction to **exercise 4** on **p.23** of the main course-book.

- Preparation: revise the vocabulary and structures from the *Hilfe* box on **p.23** of the main course-book, stressing vocabulary such as *Sportmöglichkeiten* and *ein Schloss* which is relevant for the description of the picture.
- Students study the picture and jot down key words to describe the town.
- Less able students can work in pairs, using a dictionary where necessary.
- Elicit from the class features which they can see in the picture:
  T: *Was gibt es in der Stadt?*
  S: *Ein Schloss!* etc.
  or, with less able students:
  T: *Hat die Stadt viele Sportmöglichkeiten?* etc.
- Students write out their descriptions in full sentences. This can be set as a homework task.
- Less able students can be provided with a list of relevant vocabulary, or sentence halves to match together.
- Correct students' written answers individually.

Du bist dran!

Page 21

The tasks on this page provide basic revision of the topic of town and local surroundings from **Teil 1** of the main course-book.

1 Fragen und Antworten

This task introduces the students to relevant questions and answers by means of a matching exercise. Their answers to this task will then provide a model for task 3 below.

2 Mach mit!

This reading task provides an introduction or alternative to **exercise 5** on **p.23** of the main course-book.

- Students identify both positive and negative features in Mustafa's description of his town.
- Follow-up: students undertake a similar analysis of their town.
- Less able students decide which of Mustafa's sentences apply to their own town and amend those that do not. Alternatively, they are provided with a list of statements in a scrambled list to sort into negative and positive.

3 Jetzt bist du dran!

Students record themselves speaking about their town. More able students should try to create a continuous account, whilst less able students

TEIL 1

could work in pairs, with one person asking the questions and the other responding; they then swap roles.

D Der Tagesablauf

Page 22

1 Wie spät ist es?

This listening task revises time expressions and will serve as an alternative or introduction to **exercise 1** on **p.28** of the main course-book.

- Preparation: revise saying what the time is. If using a clock to revise time, bear in mind that less able students generally find digital time easier to read than analogue.
- Preparation: students work in pairs, groups or teams, with one student/team giving the time in English and another giving it in German.
- Students listen to the recording and match the times to their written form.
- With less able learners, play the recording in short sections.
- Answers can be checked in pairs.
- Follow-up: students play a game to practise time expressions. Student 1 says a time to student 2, student 2 gives the time quarter of an hour later, and so on round the class:
  S1: *Viertel vor sieben!*
  S2: *Sieben Uhr!*
  S3: *Viertel nach sieben!* etc.
  The game can be repeated with different time intervals (half an hour, ten minutes, etc.).

> **Transcript**
> 1 – Mutti! Wie spät ist es?
>   – Es ist halb drei.
> 2 – Und wie spät ist es jetzt?
>   – Ach, Björn, es ist Viertel nach vier.
> 3 – Katrin, wie spät ist es?
>   – Wie spät? Es ist halb acht.
> 4 – Wie spät ist es, Herr Frank?
>   – Es ist drei Uhr.
> 5 – Entschuldigung! Wie spät ist es?
>   – Es ist Viertel nach sechs.
> 6 – Wie spät ist es, Sabina?
>   – Es ist fünf Uhr.

2 Wie sieht der Alltag aus?

This matching task will serve as a simpler alternative or introduction to **exercise 2** on **p.28** of the main course-book. It revises structures and vocabulary for talking about daily routine.

- Preparation: revise the key vocabulary and structures to describe daily routine.
- Students match the sentences and pictures.
- Answers can be checked in pair-work, group-work or a whole-class session.
- Follow-up: this task lends itself to a variety of follow-up tasks including:
- Students use this routine as a model for their own, simply changing times as appropriate. The more able students should be encouraged to change times and the sequence of the day's activities, or to create a weekend and weekday routine.
- Students could also draw simple pictures similar to the artwork for this task and then copy out the sentences. These can then be scrambled and students have to find matching pairs.
- The above work can also be used to create bingo cards.

3 Was fehlt?

This gap-fill task reinforces the key verbs associated with daily routine and will serve as an introduction to **exercise 2** on **p.28** of the main course-book.

- Preparation: revise the key verbs orally.
- Students complete the gap-fill, noting their answers in rough.
- More able students may be able to use the main course-book alone to help them identify the correct verbs to fill in the gaps.
- Invite students to read out their answers.
- Students write out the correct sentences in full.

Am Wochenende

Page 23

1 Frau Fleißig und Herr Faulpelz

This matching task serves as an introduction or alternative to **exercise 4** on **p.29** and **exercise 1** on **p.30** of the main course-book.

- Encourage students to note the positive features in Frau Fleißig's routine and the negative features for Herr Faulpelz. Looking at the visuals accompanying the exercises in the main course-book will assist less able students.
- Students match each statement by Frau Fleißig to the corresponding statement by Herr Faulpelz.
- Task 2 provides follow-up material.

TEIL 1

2 Ein Tag in meinem Leben

This task provides a follow-up to task 1 above. It can be completed in class or for homework.

- Students adapt phrases from task 1 and/or the main course-book to write or talk about their own daily routine.
- More able students could keep a journal for the week and compare one day with the next or a weekday with a weekend.

3 Gegenwart oder Zukunft?

This gap-filling task provides an introduction or alternative to present and future tense work on **pp.30–31** of the main course-book.

- Preparation: revise present and future tenses orally. Preparation activities could include matching tasks, substitution tasks, gap-filling with letters missing.
- Students select from the *Hilfe* box the correct verb forms to fill in the gaps.
- Students prepare their answers in rough first, either working alone or in pairs.
- Invite students to read out their answers.
- Students write out a fair copy.
- Follow-up: students write additional sentences in the present and future tenses. Alternatively, student 1 writes a list of sentences in the present tense and passes it to student 2, who rewrites it in the future and passes it to student 3, who rewrites it in the present, etc.

4 Ein Tag in der Zukunft

This writing task consolidates the ideas introduced above and provides the opportunity for students to write about their own daily routine in the future tense.

- Preparation: revise the future tense orally.
- Students adapt their answers to task 2 above in order to describe a day in the future, using the future tense.
- Less able students may find it beneficial to work in pairs. They could be provided with a list of sentences in random order as an alternative task.
- Follow-up: more able students could write about their ideal day – getting up at midday, no school, etc.

Mahlzeiten

Page 24

1 Was esse ich gern?

This simple writing task revises some basic food and drink vocabulary in preparation for **pp.32–33** in the main course-book.

- Preparation: revise key vocabulary, using visuals such as supermarket advertisements or realia such as packaging if available.
- Students rearrange the letters to make the names of the different items depicted.
- Less able students may use a dictionary to complete the task, working in pairs. They should be reminded to strike out each letter as it is used.
- Check answers as a whole-class activity. More able students may check their answers in pairs.
- Follow-up: students add *der*, *die* or *das* before each noun.

2 Was esse ich zum Frühstück?

This writing task will serve as an introduction or alternative to **exercise 2** on **p.32** of the main course-book.

- Preparation: study the picture with the whole class and elicit the names of the foods depicted. Students may use a dictionary where necessary. Alternatively, provide a longer list of foods/drinks for students to select the relevant items from.
- Students write sentences about what they have for breakfast, based on the picture.
- Less able students can be provided with a *Hilfe* list of the relevant foods and drinks in scrambled order.
- Follow-up: more able students can write about what they really eat and drink for breakfast, using a dictionary as necessary. This can be set as a homework task.

Page 25

3 Guten Appetit!

This sequencing task will serve as an introduction or easier alternative to **exercise 5** on **p.33** in the main course-book.

- Preparation: revise key vocabulary and structures, paying particular attention to word order.

- Preparation: point out to students that there is sometimes more than one acceptable answer.
- Students resequence the words to make sentences, drafting their answers in rough initially.
- Check answers as a whole-class activity.
- Students write out their answers correctly.

4 Gern oder nicht gern?

This writing task will serve as an introduction or easier alternative to **exercises 5** and **6** on **p.33** in the main course-book, and preparation for task 5 below.

- Preparation: revise the use of *ich* + verb + *gern/nicht gern*.
- Preparation: elicit from the class the German names of the foods and drinks depicted.
- Students write sentences to match the picture cues, drafting their answers in rough initially.
- Check answers as a whole-class activity.
- Students write out their answers correctly.

5 Jetzt bist du dran!

This non-directed writing task is a follow-up to task 4 above, offering students the opportunity for independent writing about their food and drink preferences.

- Preparation: brainstorm popular and unpopular foods and drinks with the class, writing up the results in two lists on the board/an OHT.
- Students write four sentences about what they like/dislike eating and drinking.
- Follow-up: task 7 below is a follow-up to this task.

6 Warum?

This task will help students to develop an understanding of correct word order in subordinate clauses, and will develop their confidence in supporting their statements with reasons using *weil*. It will serve as an introduction or easier alternative to *exercise 2c* on *p.32* of the main course-book and as preparation for task 7 below.

- Preparation: revise word order with *weil*, e.g. by demonstrating on the board/an OHT how two simple sentences can be transformed into one sentence with a main and a subordinate clause.

- Students join the sentence halves in the way which makes best sense, drafting their answers in rough initially.
- Check answers as a whole-class activity.
- Students write out the answers correctly.

7 Jetzt bist du dran!

This non-directed writing task is a follow-up to tasks 5 and 6 above.

- Students add *weil*-clauses to their work for task 5.
- Less able students use/adapt the *weil*-clauses from their answers to task 6 above.
- Follow-up: this task could form the basis of an illustrated poster or web page.

E Schulfächer

Page 26

1 Kreuzworträtsel

This crossword is designed to be a light-hearted activity, providing some basic revision of school subjects and reinforcing the need for accuracy of spelling.

- Preparation: practise school subjects orally: T: *Was ist „geography" auf Deutsch? Was ist „Geschichte" auf Englisch?* etc.
- Preparation: check that students understand the symbols.
- Preparation: practice the German alphabet orally to reinforce German spellings. Alternatively, a game of Hangman could be used.
- Students complete the crossword in German.
- To check answers, either provide a correct version on an OHT, or draw the outline on the board and complete it according to the class's instructions.
- Follow-up: students create their own crosswords using symbols or English/German clues. Alternatively they design wordsearches. Provide squared paper and encourage neatness and accuracy. The best crosswords/wordsearches could be copied and used as a resource.

2 Ich mag Chemie!

This listening task will serve as an introduction or alternative to **exercise 1b** on **p.34** of the main course-book.

TEIL 1

- Preparation: revise expressing likes and dislikes orally. Students can practise in pairs or in direct response to your questions.
- Students listen to the recording and complete the table according to Arturo's likes and dislikes.
- With less able learners, play the recording in short sections.
- Follow-up: more able students can attempt **exercise 1b** on **p.34** of the main course-book.

Transcript

– Also, Arturo, welche Schulfächer magst du, und welche magst du nicht?
– Zuerst die Fächer, die ich mag! Chemie finde ich wirklich toll und unser Chemielehrer ist super. Aber mein Lieblingsfach ist Physik und ich möchte später Physik studieren. Fremdsprachen gefallen mir auch: Wir lernen an unserer Schule Englisch und Französisch. Ich habe Französisch gewählt, weil ich in den Ferien mit meinen Eltern nach Frankreich fahre. Ach ja, Erdkunde und Informatik sind auch okay und Musik auch! Geschichte – na ja, ich weiß nicht, manchmal ist der Unterricht furchtbar langweilig. Die Fächer, die ich überhaupt nicht mag, sind Mathe, Biologie und Sport. Unser Mathelehrer ist furchtbar streng und er gibt uns immer zu viele Hausaufgaben auf. Ehrlich – Mathe, nein danke! Biologie ist echt schwierig, aber Sport ist noch schlimmer. Ich bin total unsportlich!

3 Meine Schulfächer

a This writing task consolidates the ideas introduced above and provides the opportunity for students to express in writing their own views using the *Hilfe* box provided. Students are required not only to say whether they like a subject or not but also to give a reason for their view.

- Preparation: introduce the additional vocabulary. Students may find it helpful to design a symbol to accompany each new word, or this can be undertaken as a class project.
- Students jot down answers in rough initially.
- Invite students to read out their answers. More able students should be encouraged to give their answers as full sentences, whilst less able may require model sentences to copy and fill in, using the key words from their initial notes.
- Students copy out their own answers correctly as a homework task.

Meine Schule

Page 27

1 Wie ist deine Schule?

This matching task will serve as an introduction or alternative to **exercise 1** on **p.36** of the main course-book by encouraging initial recognition of the sentences given in the course-book *Hilfe* box.

- Students match the descriptions provided with the correct visual.
- Check answers as a whole-class activity: T: *Was ist Bild a?* etc.
- Alternatively, students could work in pairs or small groups and be encouraged to question and answer each other in a similar way.

2 Stephanie beschreibt ihre Schule

a This listening gap-fill task complements task 1 above.

- Students listen to the recording and fill in the gaps in the model letter using the *Hilfe* box to ensure accurate spellings.
- With less able students, play the recording in short sections.

Transcript

Meine Schule heißt Franz-Gruber-Schule. Meine Schule ist modern. Sie ist sehr groß und liegt auf dem Land. Meine Schule ist eine Gesamtschule. Sie ist gemischt. Wir haben Jungen und Mädchen. Die meisten Schüler sind fleißig, aber einige sind faul. Die meisten Lehrer sind freundlich.

b This guided writing task is a follow-up to task 2a above.

- Students write a letter in German describing their school, along similar lines to Stephanie's letter. They should refer to the *Hilfe* box on **p.36** of the main course-book for alternative words.
- Less able students use Stephanie's letter as a template for their writing.
- More able students should be encouraged to produce a more independent piece of writing.
- Follow-up: students can produce a cassette about their school. This could either be a monologue of five or six sentences, or a short interview.

Zukunft in der Schule

1 Was sind deine Pläne für das nächste Schuljahr?

This writing task will serve as an introduction or a more structured alternative to exercise 3b on p.39 of the main course-book.

- Preparation: elicit key words to describe each of the pictures:
  T: *Bild a: Was macht er/sie?* etc.
- Preparation: revise the formation of the future tense.
- Students write sentences in the future tense about their plans, based on the picture cues. They draft their answers in rough initially.
- Check answers as a whole-class activity.
- Students write up a fair copy for homework.

Du bist dran!

Page 28

The tasks on this page provide basic revision of the topic of school from **Teil 1** of the main course-book.

1 Fragen und Antworten

This task introduces students to relevant questions and answers by means of a matching exercise. This will then provide model answers for task 3 below.

2 Mach mit!

This is a writing exercise in which students unscramble the words to complete Katrin's description of her school. Key words are provided to assist students.

- Less able students may begin matching by counting letters in the anagrams and the key words box to find matches or by noting similar letters.
- More able students should be encouraged to think of words that might fit or be appropriate and only then look for the word in the key words box.
- Ensure that students understand the meaning of the letter before they attempt the follow-up homework task below.
- Students write about themselves in a similar way for homework.

3 Jetzt bist du dran!

Students prepare and record their own model answers along similar lines to task 1 above, using **pp.36–37** of the main course-book for reference. More able students should try to create a continuous account, whilst less able students could work in pairs with one student asking the questions and the other responding; they then swap roles.

Kontrolle 1: Hören

Page 29

This section consists of three listening tests to measure students' understanding of a range of material covered in **Teil 1**.

1 Students match the three faces to the recorded descriptions.

> **Transcript**
> 1 Ich heiße Silvia. Ich habe kurze, lockige, blonde Haare. Ich habe eine kleine Nase und ich trage gern große Ohrringe. Ich trage auch eine Brille.
> 2 Ich heiße Albert. Ich habe fast keine Haare. Ich habe eine Glatze. Ich habe einen schwarzen Schnurrbart. Ich trage auch eine Brille.
> 3 Ich heiße Ute. Ich habe lange, glatte, braune Haare. Ich trage auch eine Brille! Ich trage gern Ohrringe, aber in meiner Nase!

2 Students identify the school subjects and indicate whether Karl likes them or not. You may wish to warn students that some of the subjects given in the workbook are not mentioned in the recording.

> **Transcript**
> – Also, Karl. Morgen muss ich zum Elternabend in der Schule. Erzähl mir ein bisschen was über deine Fächer. Wie findest du Mathe?
> – Mathe? Also … ähm … Mathe finde ich eigentlich ziemlich schwer – das verstehe ich nicht sehr gut! Aber Deutsch! – Deutsch ist super! Ich lese sehr gern und es gibt so viele interessante Bücher und die Lehrerin ist sehr nett und …
> – Aha, aber Mathe magst du nicht!
> – Ähm … nein!
> – Okay! Und sonst? Fremdsprachen? Wie findest du Englisch?
> – Hmm, Englisch gefällt mir gut.

TEIL 1

> – Und Naturwissenschaften? Magst du Biologie?
> – Nein!! Biologie ist langweilig! Aber Chemie … na ja, Chemie ist echt toll!!
> – Chemie, Deutsch und Englisch magst du also sehr gern.
> – Nicht sehr gern, aber ziemlich gern!
> – Alles klar! Aber Mathe und Biologie nicht!
> – Nein!

3 Students identify aspects of a weekend routine in the perfect tense and place the visuals relating to it in the correct order.

> **Transcript**
> – Hallo, Monika! Hier ist Karla. Wie geht's?
> – Gut, danke! Was hast du denn am Samstag gemacht?
> – Also, ich bin um acht Uhr aufgestanden und habe ein bisschen ferngesehen.
> – Im Bett?
> – Na klar! Dann habe ich um 10 Uhr mit Caro Tennis gespielt. Natürlich habe ich gewonnen!
> – He! Toll!
> – Ja, und nachmittags habe ich zu Hause Musik gehört.
> – Schön! Und abends? Hast du Paul gesehen?
> – Ja! Ich habe mit Maia einen Hamburger in der Imbissstube gegessen und er war da!! Er hat mich gesehen, glaube ich!
> – He, prima! Und hast du auch was zu ihm gesagt? …

Kontrolle 2: Sprechen

Page 30

This section consists of four speaking tests to measure students' understanding of a range of material covered in **Teil 1**.

1 Students use the profile provided as a basis for a description of themselves. They record the description on cassette for assessment purposes.

2 Students describe what they do/do not like doing, based on the visuals.

3 Students record a description of the town depicted in the visual.

4 Students describe the two rooms depicted in the visuals.

Kontrolle 3: Lesen

Page 31

This section consists of three reading tests to measure students' understanding of a range of material covered in **Teil 1**.

1 Students read the profile and insert the relevant details from the boxes.

2 Students read the sentences underneath each visual and decide whether the description for each visual is correct or not.

- More able students should be encouraged to correct those sentences that they consider to be incorrect.

3 Students read the longer reading passage and decide whether the places and facilities are present in the town in question or not.

- Less able students will require advice on skimming for key words. Point out that they need not understand every word of the text
- More able students may wish to attempt an analysis and/or description of their town, real or imaginary, in addition to the set task.

Kontrolle 4: Schreiben

Page 32

This section consists of four writing tests to measure students' understanding of a range of material covered in Teil 1.

1 Students are asked to complete the e-mail by filling in the gaps.

- More able students may wish to use this gapped text as a model for a text of their own in addition to the set task.

2 The ten visuals depict Richard's daily routine. Students write a sentence for each visual in the present tense.

3 Students write the ten sentences in the perfect tense.

4 Students describe the room depicted in the visual using appropriate vocabulary and prepositions with the dative.

- More able students may wish to describe their own room in addition to the set task.
- Less able students could design a room, perhaps using ICT, and then describe it.

TEIL 2

A Wie komme ich zum Busbahnhof? –

Page 34

1 Wo ist … ?

This matching task will serve as an introduction to **exercise 1** on **p.46** of the main course-book.

- Preparation: practise giving and understanding directions orally, using simple diagrams on the board/an OHT, and revising the *du* imperative forms of key verbs.
- Students match the sentences to the visuals.
- Check answers as a whole-class activity, also checking that students can identify the infinitives of the imperative verb forms.
- Follow-up: more able students can put the instructions into the *Sie* imperative.

2 Wohin gehen sie?

This listening task offers further practice in listening to directions and locating the point reached on a map. It will serve as a follow-up to **exercise 1** on **p.46** of the main course-book.

- Preparation: revise the *Sie* imperative and ensure that students understand when to use *Sie* and when to use *du*.
- Students listen to the example and follow directions on the map.
- Students then listen to the next five recordings and complete the remaining maps.
- Follow-up: ask students to repeat the directions, using the maps for guidance:
  T: *Wie komme ich zur Martinskirche?* etc.

> **Transcript**
>
> a Gehen Sie geradeaus und nehmen Sie die zweite Straße links bis zur Ampel. Die Martinskirche ist rechts vom Rathaus.
> b Gehen Sie rechts bis zum Bahnhof. Biegen Sie dann links ab und nehmen Sie die erste Straße rechts. Dort ist die Bank.
> c Du gehst links am Theater vorbei und nimmst dann die vierte Straße links. Das Verkehrsamt ist auf der rechten Seite.
> d Gehen Sie links und biegen Sie dann an der Post rechts ab. Das Kino ist am Marktplatz.
> e Nehmen Sie die zweite Straße rechts und gehen Sie bis zur Ampel. Biegen Sie hier rechts ab – das Schwimmbad finden Sie auf der rechten Seite.
> f Gehen Sie bis zum Marktplatz, biegen Sie dann am Dom rechts ab. Dort ist die Post.

Page 35

3 Wie komme ich am besten … ?

This pair-work information-gap task could be used as a more guided alternative to **exercise 3** on **p.47** of the main course-book, or simply as additional practice in requesting and giving directions.

- Taking it in turns, students ask directions to the various buildings listed and mark them on their town map.

Unterwegs

Page 36

1 Schilder

This anagram task will serve as written consolidation and extension of **exercise 1** on **p.48** of the main course-book, introducing a wider range of key travel vocabulary.

- Preparation: check students' understanding of the symbols, in English if necessary.
- Students resequence the letters to make a noun to describe each symbol, and then add *der*, *die* or *das*.
- Less able students work in pairs and use a dictionary.
- Check answers as a whole-class activity, or ask more able students to check their answers in pairs.
- Follow-up: students devise further anagrams themselves, drawing symbols to illustrate their meaning.
- Follow-up: alternatively, students may wish to design a wordsearch or a crossword for travel vocabulary. The best examples can be copied and used as a resource.

2 Wo ist die nächste Bushaltestelle?

This gap-fill task will slot in at any point when working on **pp. 46–47** of the main course-book.

- Ask around the class: *Wo ist die nächste Bushaltestelle?* and point to one of the illustrations in the workbook. Students respond as appropriate: *Am/An der …*
- The written consolidation of this task will serve as a useful homework activity.

TEIL 2

Wir machen Ausflüge

Page 37

1 Ein Busfahrplan

a This aural gap-fill task will serve as a simpler alternative to **exercise 3a** on **p.50** of the main course-book.

- Preparation: revise numbers and clock times.
- Students listen to the recording and fill in the missing times on the timetable.
- Follow-up: students work in pairs, repeating the times for their partners.

Transcript

– Guten Tag. Kann ich Ihnen helfen?
– Guten Tag. Wie komme ich nach Waldeck, bitte?
– Nehmen Sie die Buslinie Nummer sechs. Die Abfahrtszeiten sind 9 Uhr, 10 Uhr 15, 11 Uhr 30, 12 Uhr 45, 14 Uhr, 15 Uhr 15, 16 Uhr 30, 17 Uhr 45, 19 Uhr und 20 Uhr 15. Die Fahrt dauert 20 Minuten.
– Muss ich umsteigen?
– Nein, der Bus fährt direkt.
– Und wo ist die nächste Bushaltestelle, bitte?
– Hier vorne am Marktplatz.
– Danke schön.
– Bitte schön.

b Students listen to the recording again and answer some simple comprehension questions. The responses should be in German but very brief.

2 Abfahrtszeiten

This listening task offers further practice of numbers and 24-hour clock times and will serve as an introduction or easier alternative to **exercise 2** on **p.50** of the main course-book.

- Preparation: revise numbers and clock times as necessary. Draw students' attention to the correct sequencing of numbers, e.g. the distinction between *fünfundneunzig* and *neunundfünfzig*.
- Preparation: call out some times and students volunteer to come to the board and write them down. Alternatively, carry out a simple dictation of times.
- Students listen to the recorded message of bus times and tick the appropriate alternative.
- Check answers as a whole-class activity.

Transcript

Die Abfahrtszeiten für die Buslinie 2 nach Berghof sind ... 7 Uhr 15 ... 9 Uhr 25 ... 11 Uhr 35 ... 13 Uhr 45 ... 15 Uhr 55 und 18 Uhr 50. Ich wiederhole ... 7 Uhr 15 ... 9 Uhr 25 ... 11 Uhr 35 ... 13 Uhr 45 ... 15 Uhr 55 und 18 Uhr 50. Vielen Dank für Ihren Anruf.

Page 38

3 Ausflug zum Tierpark

a This matching task provides further practice of clock times, this time concentrating on the conventional 12-hour clock face. It might be worth finding out how many students have traditional wrist watches of this kind and how many have those with digital clock faces. Those students used only to digital watches sometimes still struggle with conventional watch faces and times.

- Students work individually or in pairs to match up the written form of the clock time to the corresponding clock face.
- Check answers as a whole-class activity.

b Students write out the times under the clock faces. This can then serve as a record to which students refer back later.

4 Wann fährt der nächste Bus nach ... ?

This oral pair-work task provides an introduction or easier alternative to **exercise 3b** on **p.50** of the main course-book.

- Preparation: practise each section of the dialogue in turn to ensure that students understand how to follow the model.
- Preparation: give special attention to pronunciation.
- Students practise the dialogues in pairs. Monitor content and pronunciation.
- Once the task has been completed, students change roles and work through the dialogues again.
- Some students may volunteer to perform their dialogues in front of the rest of the class in a feed-back session.

B Auf dem Verkehrsamt

Page 39

1 Haben Sie … ?

This matching task consolidates **exercise 1** on **p.54** of the main course-book. It could be completed by students independently after completion of the course-book exercise.

- Preparation: present the individual items of vocabulary: *Stadtplan, Fahrplan, Broschüre über die Stadt*, etc. If possible, use realia. Stress in turn pronunciation and then correct gender.
- Preparation: combine this vocabulary with the different structures: *Haben Sie … , Ich möchte … ,* etc.
- Preparation: practise orally as a whole-class activity, then individuals practise in pairs.
- Work through **exercise 1** on **p.54** of the main course-book as a whole-class activity.
- Students complete the workbook task individually.

2 Im Verkehrsbüro

a This sequencing task develops the language acquired above and will serve as a follow-up to the listening comprehension **exercise 2** on **p.54** of the main course-book.

- Students put the dialogue in the correct sequence.
- They check their answers by completing task 2b.

b This listening task is a follow-up to task 2a.

- Students listen to the dialogue and check their own work.
- Follow-up: students write out the dialogue in full and practise it in pairs.

> **Transcript**
> – Guten Tag, kann ich Ihnen helfen?
> – Guten Tag. Haben Sie bitte eine Broschüre über die Stadt?
> – Ja, hier. Bitte sehr.
> – Danke. Was kostet das?
> – Nichts. Die Broschüre ist kostenlos.
> – Ich hätte auch gern eine Liste von Hotels.
> – Bitte sehr. Möchten Sie sonst noch etwas?
> – Ja. Ich möchte bitte einen Busfahrplan.
> – Gern. Hier, bitte.

3 Was kann man in Köln machen?

a This listening task could be used as an introduction to **exercise 3** on **p.55** of the main course-book.

- After modelling and practising the structure *Was kann man in Köln machen?* use the illustrations to elicit responses from the students as to what activities might be available: *Man kann schwimmen gehen/den Dom besuchen/ins Kino gehen,* etc.
- Students listen to the recording and tick the activities mentioned.
- Check answers as a whole-class activity.

> **Transcript**
> – Guten Tag, kann ich Ihnen helfen?
> – Ja. Ich möchte eine Broschüre über die Stadt, bitte.
> – Bitte sehr.
> – Danke. Und was kann man in Köln machen?
> – Man kann eine Stadtführung zu Fuß machen. Sie müssen unbedingt den Dom besuchen. Und wenn Sie gern einkaufen gehen, gibt es viele schöne Geschäfte.
> – Was gibt es für Kinder?
> – Es gibt einen ganz tollen Zoo am Stadtrand und auch ein Hallenbad. Und wenn Sie Lust haben, könnten Sie auch eine Schifffahrt auf dem Rhein machen.
> – Vielen Dank für Ihre Hilfe.
> – Bitte sehr.

Page 40

b Students work in pairs, using the illustrations from task 3a above to elicit responses from their partners.

c As written consolidation, students write out about five sentences based on the *Hilfe* box in task 3b above.

4 Ein Brief an das Verkehrsamt

This gap-fill writing task gives students the opportunity to practise formal letter-writing, using the language from **pp.54–55** in the main course-book.

- Students fill the gaps in pencil, using the words from the box.
- Check answers as a whole-class activity.
- Students write out the letter correctly in full. This could be completed on computer, enabling students to produce their own adapted versions.

TEIL 2

Wie waren die Ferien?

Page 41

1 Wie war das Wetter im Urlaub?

This matching task will serve as a general introduction to the weather vocabulary on **p.56** of the main course-book.

- Preparation: revise the perfect tense and the imperfect of *sein* as necessary.
- Students match up the pictures with the sentences.
- Check answers as a whole-class activity, or ask students to check their answers in pairs.

2 Wie war das Wetter?

This oral pair-work task may be used as an introduction or easier alternative to **exercise 4** on **p.56** of the main course-book.

- Students make up their own dialogues using the visual cues provided.
- Follow-up: students write down their dialogues. Less able students could create a weather chart or record sentences appropriate to the weather for that day instead.

Page 42

3 Wo warst du in den Ferien?

a This matching task introduces the basic perfect and imperfect tense structures underpinning **exercises 3–7** on **pp.56–57** of the main course-book.

- Preparation: revise the key verb forms.
- Students match up the pictures with the phrases.

b Tasks 3b and 3c may be used as an introduction or easier alternative to **exercises 6** and **7** on **p.57** of the main course-book.

- Students listen to the recording and match the pictures from 1a with the statements.
- Check answers with oral questions:
  T: *Was ist b?* etc.

> **Transcript**
>
> 1 – Vera, wo warst du letztes Jahr in den Ferien?
>   – Letztes Jahr sind wir im Winter in die Alpen gefahren – für den Skiurlaub.
> 2 – Und wo warst du letztes Jahr in den Ferien, Uwe?
>   – Letztes Jahr waren wir in Großbritannien – eine Woche in England und eine Woche in Wales.
> 3 – Anne, wo warst du voriges Jahr in den Ferien?
>   – Voriges Jahr? Voriges Jahr sind wir in die USA geflogen, für drei Wochen.
> 4 – Und du, Olaf? Wo warst du in den Ferien?
>   – Letztes Jahr waren wir in Frankreich. Wir – das sind meine Freunde Tom, Carsten und ich.
> 5 – Tanja, wo warst du in den Ferien?
>   – Also, letztes Jahr sind wir auf die Insel Sylt gefahren. Zwei Wochen Sonne – super!

c This follow-up oral pair-work task consolidates the perfect and imperfect structures covered in tasks 3a and 3b above.

- Preparation: go through the sample dialogue with the whole class.
- Students make up their own dialogues using the visuals and with the help of the vocabulary from the *Hilfe* box.
- Follow-up: students record their dialogues on cassette or in written form for homework.

Page 43

4 Wie sind sie gefahren?

This matching task reinforces key vocabulary on modes of travel, plus word order with the perfect tense.

- Students match up the pictures with the sentences and fill in the gaps with the missing information.

5 Wo haben sie gewohnt?

a This matching task reinforces key vocabulary on holiday accommodation in conjunction with the perfect tense and prepares students for task 5b.

- Students match the phrases to the illustrations.
- Check answers as a whole-class activity.

b This listening task is the follow-up to task 5a.

- Preparation: use oral practice and simple letter games to reinforce key vocabulary.
- Students listen to the recording and match the types of accommodation to the names in the table.
- Play the recording as many times as required by students, pausing after each section for less able students.

TEIL 2

- Students check their own answers in pairs by completing task 5c.

> **Transcript**
> 1 – Und wo habt ihr auf Sylt gewohnt, Tanja?
>   – Also, wir – das heißt meine Eltern und ich – haben dort in einer kleinen Pension gewohnt – direkt am Strand.
> 2 – Und du, Olaf? Wo habt ihr in Frankreich gewohnt?
>   – Meine Freunde und ich, wir haben auf einem Campingplatz gewohnt, in der Nähe von Avignon.
> 3 – Anne, wo habt ihr in den Ferien gewohnt?
>   – Wir haben in einem großen Ferienapartment gewohnt, in Florida – nur 10 Minuten von Disneyworld entfernt!
> 4 – Und du, Uwe? Wo hast du in Großbritannien gewohnt?
>   – Wir? Wir haben in einer Jugendherberge übernachtet – eine Woche in Devon und dann eine Woche in Cardiff.
> 5 – Vera, wo habt ihr in den Ferien gewohnt?
>   – Meine Familie und ich – wir haben in einem Hotel, also einem Ski-Hotel gewohnt, ganz in der Nähe von St. Moritz.

c This oral pair-work task consolidates the vocabulary and structures covered in task 5b above and allows students to check their own answers in pairs.

- Preparation: revise perfect-tense word order in questions and answers.
- Working in pairs, students use their answers to task 5b to make dialogues.
- Less able students could record their dialogues to help them with task 5d.

d Students consolidate the language practised in task 5 by writing sentences based on their dialogues.

C Ich habe ein Zimmer reserviert

Page 44

1 Haben Sie ein Zimmer frei?

a This matching task will serve as an introduction to **exercise 2** on **p.58** of the main course-book.

- Preparation: use the visuals to present or revise basic hotel-related vocabulary.
- Students match the recorded requests to the visuals.

> **Transcript**
> 1 Guten Morgen! Ich suche ein Doppelzimmer mit Dusche und WC.
> 2 Guten Tag! Ich möchte bitte ein Einzelzimmer mit Bad und WC.
> 3 Haben Sie bitte ein Einzelzimmer mit Dusche, WC und Fernseher?
> 4 Guten Tag! Ich suche ein Einzelzimmer mit Dusche und WC.
> 5 Ich möchte ein Doppelzimmer mit WC, Bad und Balkon.
> 6 Ich suche ein Doppelzimmer mit Dusche, WC und Telefon.

b On completing the listening exercise, the visuals form the basis for further oral practice as a whole-class or pair-work activity.

2 Ich möchte ein Zimmer reservieren

This matching task will serve as an introduction to **Unit 2C** or as written consolidation after **exercises 4** and **5** on **p.59** of the main course-book.

- Students match the German phrases to their English equivalents.
- Follow-up: this task could be extended into an ongoing phrase book to which students may add as the course progresses. It could be compiled on computer.

Page 45

3 Welches Hotel?

This reading task will serve as a follow-up to **exercises 1** and **2** on **p.58** of the main course-book. It requires students to scan short authentic texts for specific information.

- Preparation: go through the sample answer with the whole class. Emphasise that students do not have to understand every word of the adverts in order to complete the exercise.
- Students read the statements in the speech bubbles. Make sure that they understand the statements before proceeding with the task.
- Students read the brief adverts for the three hotels. They select one or possibly two hotels which match the requirements expressed in each speech bubble.
- Less able students work in pairs or in small groups.
- Check answers as a whole-class activity, with some students reading the requests and others making the appropriate recommendations: *Ich empfehle …* , etc.

TEIL 2

4 Hotelreservierungen

This listening task will serve as an introduction or easier alternative to **exercise 4** on **p.59** of the main course-book.

- Students listen to the recorded messages requesting hotel accommodation and make notes on the booking sheets. They should pencil in their answers initially.
- Check answers as a whole-class activity.
- Students write up their answers correctly.
- Follow-up: base some class oral work on the results:
  T: *Was möchte Herr Dorn?/Wie viele Nächte möchte Frau Schwarz?* etc.
- Follow-up: using additional completed 'booking forms', students work in pairs to make their own recorded messages.

Transcript

1 Guten Tag! Mein Name ist Dorn – D-O-R-N. Ich möchte bitte ein Einzelzimmer für drei Nächte vom ersten bis zum vierten August reservieren. Danke.
2 Guten Morgen! Meyer ist mein Name. M-E-Y-E-R. Ich suche ein Doppelzimmer für zwei Nächte vom zehnten bis zum zwölften September.
3 Hallo! Mein Name ist Frau Schwarz – S-C-H-W-A-R-Z – und ich suche ein Einzelzimmer für eine Woche – also sieben Nächte vom zweiten bis zum neunten Juli.
4 Guten Tag! Mein Name ist Klein – K-L-E-I-N. Ich möchte bitte ein Doppelzimmer für drei Nächte vom einundzwanzigsten bis zum vierundzwanzigsten Juni. Danke schön.

Page 46

5 Herr Schmidt reserviert ein Zimmer

a This sequencing task provides further practice in booking a hotel room and will serve as an alternative or as a follow-up to **exercise 5** on **p.59** of the main course-book. It could also usefully be set as a homework task.

- Students select from the *Hilfe* box the correct responses to complete the dialogue. This could be done orally in the first instance as a whole-class activity or the responses numbered or pencilled in by students individually.
- Check answers as a whole-class activity.

b Once the dialogue is completed, students practise the dialogue in pairs. They then make up their own versions based on the original.

6 Schriftliche Reservierungen

This writing task will serve as a more structured alternative to **exercise 6** on **p.59** of the main course-book.

- Preparation: work through the sample answer by asking simple oral questions based on its content:
  T: *Wie viele Zimmer möchten sie?/Wann möchten sie die Zimmer reservieren?/Wie viele Nächte bleiben sie?* etc.
- Students write three letters using the information in the grid and the model letter provided. The task could be completed on computer.

Am Campingplatz

Page 47

1 Haben Sie noch Platz?

This matching task provides some basic revision of the key phrases from this topic.

- Students match up the questions with the answers.
- Check answers as a whole-class activity.
- Follow-up: to provide reinforcement for the less able, use an OHT or the board to provide alternative sentences to match to questions.

2 Was sagen die Touristen?

a This listening task may be used as an introduction or easier alternative to **exercise 1** on **p.60** of the main course-book.

- Students listen to the recording and find the correct pictures.
- Check answers as a whole-class activity.
- Follow-up: as homework, students write out the question and as many alternative answers as possible, or record one or more mini-dialogues.

Transcript

1 – Guten Tag, haben Sie noch Platz für eine Nacht?
  – Für wie viele Personen?
  – Für zwei Erwachsene und zwei Kinder.
  – Haben Sie ein Zelt?
  – Ja, wir haben ein Zelt.
2 – Haben Sie noch Platz, bitte?
  – Für wie viele Nächte?
  – Für zwei Nächte.
  – Und für wie viele Personen?

TEIL 2

> – Für einen Erwachsenen und zwei Kinder. Und wir haben ein Wohnmobil.
> 3 – Haben Sie noch Platz?
> – Für wie viele Nächte?
> – Für eine Nacht. Und für einen Erwachsenen und ein Kind.
> – Haben Sie ein Zelt?
> – Nein, wir haben einen Wohnwagen.
> 4 – Guten Tag! Ja, bitte?
> – Sagen Sie, haben Sie noch Platz – für zwei Nächte?
> – Ja, für wie viele Personen?
> – Für zwei Erwachsene und ein Kind. Wir haben ein Zelt.

b This oral pair-work task may be used as an introduction or easier alternative to **exercise 3** on **p.61** of the main course-book.

- Students make up their own dialogues with the help of the visual cues from task 2a.
- Follow-up: students can record their dialogues on cassette or practise the task in writing.
- Follow-up: less able students could use model letters, postcards or fill in gaps in a model letter before writing their own letters/postcards, with or without visual support.

In der Jugendherberge

Page 48

1 Was sagen die Gäste?

This matching task reinforces key vocabulary for this topic and can be used in conjunction with **exercise 1** on **p.62** of the main course-book.

- Students match up the phrases with the pictures.

2 Jasmin schreibt einen Brief an die Jugendherberge Seetal

a This listening task serves as revision/practice for the follow-up writing task 2b.

- Students listen to the recording and fill in the missing words.
- Less able students can be provided with the missing words on the board/OHT in jumbled order. If the words are numbered, students can initially insert the numbers in the gaps. They can then copy out the words in full after listening to the recording.
- Check answers as a whole-class activity.
- Students write out the complete letter. If this is done on computer, the completed letter can easily be used as a template for task 2b.

> **Transcript**
> Birmingham, 13. März … Sehr geehrte Damen und Herren … wir möchten vom 5. Mai bis 7. Mai für zwei Nächte in Ihrer Jugendherberge übernachten. … Wir sind ein Mädchen und zwei Jungen. …
> Wir hätten gern Halbpension. … Mit freundlichen Grüßen … Jasmin Claaßens

b This task revises the writing of reservation letters (cf. **exercise 6** on **p.59** of the main course-book) in the context of a visit to a youth hostel.

- Preparation: remind students of the key features of a formal letter, with reference to task 2a.
- Students write a reservation letter, using the picture cues.
- Less able students use their letters from task 2a as a template.
- Follow-up: students produce their own versions (preferably on computer) with different booking details. They could work in pairs, with one student producing picture cues and the other adapting the letter accordingly. Students then swap roles.

3 Was ist das Problem?

This matching activity can be used as an introduction/easier alternative to **exercise 3** on **p.63** of the main course-book.

- Students match the phrases to the pictures.

D Auf Urlaub

Page 49

1 Bonner Attraktionen

This matching task reinforces key vocabulary for this topic and prepares students for writing task 2 below.

- Students match the pictures to the sentences.
- Follow-up: Ask students questions about their own town, based on the statements in task 1 (this will serve as a preparation for task 2 below):
  T: *Gibt es in X viele Sehenswürdigkeiten?* etc.

2 Meine Stadt

This writing task may be used as an alternative to **exercise 3** on **p.68** of the main course-book.

- Students prepare and write a simple brochure for their own town, using task 1 above as a model.
- Students could be referred to local authority websites as a source of photos of local attractions/features for use in their brochure.
- Students may prefer to present their texts as a web page or as a poster.
- Less able students could be provided with a gapped text to complete.
- Follow-up: students produce a short promotional cassette based on their text, perhaps incorporating music of their choice.

Page 50

This page focuses on the perfect tense and provides tasks which may be used as an introduction or easier alternative to the exercises on **p.69** of the main course-book. They may also be used in conjunction with **Grammatik 2a** on **pp.64–65** of the main course-book.

3 Was haben sie im Urlaub gemacht?

- Students unscramble the perfect tense sentences and write them down correctly.
- Check answers as a whole-class activity.
- Follow-up: students use sentences from **exercises 4** and **5b** on **p.69** of the main course-book and scramble them for each other.

4 Urlaub in Österreich

This gap-fill task is an easier alternative to **exercise 3** on **p.65** of the main course-book.

- Students fill in the gaps with the correct past participles provided and underline key parts of the sentence.
- Check answers and comprehension of the text as a whole-class activity.

Du bist dran! Gegenwart und Zukunft

Page 51

This page deals with descriptions of holidays in the present tense and the use of the present with time phrases to indicate future plans. With the help of this framework, students can produce a large number of sentences. The diagram may be used as the basis for oral or written work.

- Preparation: you may wish to work on each speech bubble separately initially, revising vocabulary, checking knowledge of genders and indicating the sections of the main course-book from which each item has come.
- Less able students may find it useful to create their own version of this diagram in English for reference and assistance when producing sentences orally or in writing. Speech bubbles could be tackled individually for homework or as a comprehension checking device once revision has been completed in class.
- Once the individual questions and responses have been understood and practised, they can serve as a starting-point for the following ideas:
- Writing tasks: postcards and letters to friends back home – both negative (i.e. complaining) and positive; holiday diary or web page, using travel brochures or tourist websites as a source of pictures.
- Oral tasks: simple narratives about holiday plans; answerphone messages to friends; a monologue by an over-enthusiastic tour guide. Taped commentaries could also form a verbal record to accompany any of the writing tasks above.
- Least able students, for whom written work is difficult, may benefit from this page being put on the computer network. Students could then cut and paste from this resource to create their own work.

Du bist dran! Vergangenheit

Page 52

This page deals with descriptions of holidays in the perfect and the imperfect tense. With the help of this framework, students can produce a large number of sentences.

The diagram may be used as the basis for oral or written work.

- Preparation: you may wish to work on each speech bubble separately initially, revising vocabulary, checking knowledge of genders and indicating the sections of the main course-book from which each item has come.
- Less able students may find it useful to create their own version of this diagram in English for reference and assistance when producing sentences orally or in writing. Speech bubbles

could be tackled individually for homework or as a comprehension checking device once revision has been completed in class.

- Once the individual questions and responses have been understood and practised, they can serve as a starting-point for the following ideas:
- Writing tasks: postcards and letters to friends back home – both negative (i.e. complaining) and positive; holiday diary or web page, using travel brochures or tourist websites as a source of pictures.
- Oral tasks: simple narratives about holiday plans; answerphone messages to friends; a monologue by an over-enthusiastic tour guide. Taped commentaries could also form a verbal record to accompany any of the writing tasks above.
- Least able students, for whom written work is difficult, may benefit from this page being put on the computer network. Students could then cut and paste from this resource to create their own work.

Essen und Trinken

Page 53

1 Was isst du gern? Was trinkst du gern?

This writing task revises the structure *Ich esse/trinke (nicht) gern ...* with some basic foods and drinks, and may be used as an introduction to **exercises 1** and **2** on **p.70** of the main course-book.

- Students write sentences in response to the picture cues.
- Less able students may be provided with key words in scrambled order.

2 Im Café an der Ecke

This pair-work task provides the opportunity for some free oral practice based in a café context.

- Preparation: work through the items in the illustration, spending time on correct pronunciation.
- Students practise the sample dialogue as a whole-class activity (the class could be divided into two groups A and B) and in pairs.
- Students work in pairs to create their own dialogues, taking it in turns to play the roles of customer and waiter.
- Follow-up: students perform their dialogues to the rest of the class or record them on tape.

Zahlen, bitte!

1 Kannst du mir bitte ... reichen?

This simple matching task will serve as an introduction or easier alternative to **exercise 1a** on **p.72** of the main course-book.

- Students match the nouns to the items in the picture.
- Follow-up: as a whole-class activity, elicit the accusative forms in a sentence context: Kannst du mir bitte *den/die/das/einen/eine/ein* ... reichen?

Auf der Bank und Post

Page 54

1 Wörter und Zahlen

This matching task provides basic revision of numbers and is a useful introduction to **Unit 2E**.

- Students match numbers in written form to their numerical equivalent.
- Check answers as a whole-class activity.
- Follow-up: students create two sets of cards, one with the written form and the other with the numerical form, to be matched up as a card game.

2 Zahlen, Zahlen!

This writing/reading task provides further numbers practice in a different form and will again serve as a useful introductory exercise to **Unit 2E**. Alternatively, it could be set as a homework task.

- Students write out the numbers in written form.

3 Auf der Bank

This matching task offers additional practice of transactional language in a bank context and may be used in conjunction with **exercises 1–3** on **p.74** of the main course-book. It might also serve as a useful follow-up task to be completed at home.

- Preparation: revise the key vocabulary in the speech bubbles.
- Students work alone or in pairs to match questions to answers.
- Check the solution as a whole-class activity.
- Students practise the dialogue in pairs.

TEIL 2

Page 55

4 Post-Worträtsel

This task concentrates on the basic vocabulary used in post office transactions in preparation for **exercises 5–7** on **p.75** of the main course-book.

a This is an anagram task.

- Preparation: with less able students, start with the illustrations in task 4b and ask students to name them in German:
T: *Wie heißt „letter" auf Deutsch?* etc.
Better still, bring in some props (letters, postcards, parcels, etc.) and use these to ensure that vocabulary has been learnt and understood.
- Students work individually or in pairs to unjumble the words.

b This is a simple matching task.

- Students match each unjumbled word from task 4a to the correct illustration.
- Once each word has been matched to an illustration, students write the correct form of the word.

5 Auf der Post

This writing or speaking task is a simpler version of **exercise 6** on **p.75** of the main course-book.

- Preparation: drill the structures in the *Hilfe* box, paying special attention to pronunciation.
- Students produce sentences using the picture cues. The task can be completed orally (as pair-work) or in written form (individually).

Mir geht's nicht gut

Page 56

1 Ich muss zum Arzt!

This matching task serves as an introduction to **exercises 1 and 2** on **p.76** of the main course-book.

- Preparation: practise the key vocabulary and structures with the help of mime or visuals
- Students match the pictures to the phrases.

2 Ich möchte einen Termin

This multiple-choice listening task can be used in conjunction with **exercises 2** and **3** on **pp.76–77** of the main coursebook.

- Students listen to the recording in sections and choose the correct answers.
- Follow-up: less able students consolidate the listening by writing out simplified dialogues made up of three or four sentences.

> **Transcript**
>
> A – Praxis Dr. Stein, guten Morgen!
> – Guten Morgen! Ich hätte gern einen Termin mit Frau Dr. Stein.
> – Wie ist dein Name, bitte?
> – Thorsten Lemke.
> – Und was fehlt dir, Thorsten?
> – Also, ich habe seit zwei Tagen Bauchschmerzen.
> – Und hast du auch Fieber?
> – Ja, ich habe auch Fieber.
> – Gut, wir haben heute Nachmittag noch einen Termin frei.
> – Und um wie viel Uhr?
> – Um 17 Uhr.
> – Ja, das geht in Ordnung. Vielen Dank und auf Wiederhören!
> B – Guten Morgen, Praxis Dr. Stein.
> – Guten Morgen! Ich hätte gern einen Termin.
> – Was fehlt Ihnen denn?
> – Ich habe starke Ohrenschmerzen. Und mein Hals tut weh.
> – Moment bitte ... passt Ihnen morgen um 15 Uhr?
> – Ja, vielen Dank.
> – So, dann brauche ich noch Ihren Namen.
> – Mein Name ist Andrea Seemann – S-E-E-M-A-N-N.
> – Gut, Frau Seemann, bis morgen. Auf Wiederhören!
> – Auf Wiederhören!

3 Beim Arzt

This listening task can be used with **exercise 3** on **p.77** of the main course-book.

- Students listen to the recording and choose the correct prescriptions.

> **Transcript**
>
> – Guten Tag, Frau Doktor.
> – Guten Tag, Andreas. Wo tut's denn weh?
> – Mein Rücken tut weh, Frau Doktor! Ich war gestern zu lange in der Sonne.
> – Hmm, das sieht wirklich schlimm aus. Du hast Sonnenbrand. Hast du auch Fieber?
> – Nein, aber mir ist schlecht.
> – Gut, ich gebe dir ein Rezept für Salbe zum Einreiben.
> – Vielen Dank, Frau Doktor! Auf Wiedersehen!
> – Auf Wiedersehen.

> - Guten Tag, Ulla, was fehlt dir denn?
> - Tag, Frau Doktor. Au, mein Finger tut so weh! Ich habe mir in den Finger geschnitten.
> - Ich schaue mal …
> - Aua! Muss ich ins Krankenhaus?
> - Nein, so schlimm ist es nicht. Ich mache dir einen Verband.
> - Und für die Schmerzen?
> - Ich gebe dir ein Rezept für Schmerztabletten. Hier, bitte.
> - Vielen Dank.

Page 57

4 Wie geht's?

a This oral pair-work task is a follow-up to tasks 1–3 above.

- Students make up their own dialogues with the help of the visual cues provided.
- Students could act out their dialogues in front of the class or record them on tape.

b This oral pair-work task is more open-ended than task 4a.

- In pairs, students act out different ailments which their partners have to guess.

5 In der Apotheke

a This matching task reinforces the key vocabulary necessary for task 5b.

- Students match up the pictures with the information.

b This listening task may be used as an introduction or easier alternative to **exercise 3** on **p.77** of the main course-book.

- Preparation: check students' understanding of the ailments and remedies orally before playing the recording.
- Students listen to the recording and match the pictures from task 4a to the speakers.
- Check answers as a whole-class activity.

> **Transcript**
> 1 – So, hier sind Ihre Tabletten gegen Magenschmerzen.
> – Danke. Wie oft muss ich die Tabletten nehmen?
> – Nehmen Sie die Tabletten dreimal täglich vor den Mahlzeiten.
> – Dreimal am Tag vor den Mahlzeiten – gut.
> 2 – Ihr Hustensaft – bitte sehr.
> – Danke sehr. Wie oft muss ich den Hustensaft nehmen?
> – Nehmen Sie vor dem Schlafengehen einen Esslöffel.
> – Einen Esslöffel?
> – Ja.
> 3 – So, hier sind Ihre Tropfen gegen Augenschmerzen.
> – Ja, danke. Wie oft soll ich die Tropfen nehmen?
> – Alle vier Stunden.
> – Und wie viele Tropfen?
> – Einen Tropfen in jedes Auge.

c This guided pair-work task provides oral consolidation of tasks 5a and 5b above.

- Preparation: practise dialogues with the class first:
  A: *Hier sind Ihre Tabletten.*
  B: *Wie oft muss ich die Tabletten nehmen?*
  A: *Nehmen Sie die Tabletten dreimal täglich.*
  B: *Vielen Dank. Auf Wiedersehen!*
- Students make up their own dialogues with the information provided in task 5a.
- Follow-up: students record their own dialogues about illnesses and remedies.

Hilfe!

Page 58

1 Was haben sie verloren?

This matching task revises the key vocabulary for **exercises 4–6** on **p.79** of the main course-book.

- Students match up the pictures with the correct nouns.

2 Ich habe meine Tasche verloren!

This oral pair-work task may be used as an introduction or easier alternative to **exercise 5** on **p.79** of the main course-book.

- Students make up their own dialogues in pairs using the visual cues and the *Hilfe* box provided.
- Follow-up: students consolidate their work by writing out three dialogues for homework.

Kontrolle 1: Hören

Page 59

This section consists of two listening tests to measure students' understanding of a range of material covered in **Teil 2**.

TEIL 2

1 Students listen to Herr Braun making a reservation at Hotel Schöneck. For each of the three questions 1–3, students select the correct response.

Transcript

– Guten Morgen. Hotel Schöneck. Kann ich Ihnen helfen?
– Guten Morgen. Mein Name ist Braun – B-R-A-U-N. Ich möchte ein Zimmer reservieren, bitte.
– Aha. Was für ein Zimmer hätten Sie gern, Herr Braun?
– Ich hätte gern ein Einzelzimmer mit WC und Dusche.
– Ja. Ein Einzelzimmer mit WC und Dusche. Haben Sie noch andere Wünsche? Möchten Sie zum Beispiel ein Zimmer mit Balkon oder vielleicht einen Fernseher oder ein Telefon im Zimmer?
– Ein Zimmer mit Fernseher wäre schön.
– Aha. Und wann möchten Sie das Zimmer, bitte?
– Vom 13. bis zum 30. August, bitte.
– Gut. Mit Fernseher. Vom 13. bis zum 30. August. Geht in Ordnung!
– Vielen Dank. Auf Wiederhören!
– Auf Wiederhören!

2 Students listen to people complaining about injuries. They write the appropriate number in each box on the sketch.

Transcript

1 – Oh, ich muss mich hinsetzen!
– Was fehlt dir denn?
– Mein Rücken tut mir schrecklich weh!
– Dann leg dich sofort aufs Sofa und ich bringe dir eine Tasse Tee.
– Oh, danke schön. Das mache ich gleich.
2 – Nein. Entschuldigung. Ich kann nicht mehr spielen!
– Warum denn nicht? Ich habe das Spiel fast gewonnen!
– Es ist mein Knie. Mein Knie tut furchtbar weh. Tut mir Leid, aber es geht heute nicht mehr.
– Okay. Wie du willst! Wir spielen morgen wieder.
3 – Oh! Das tut weh!
– Was ist los, Vati?
– Ich habe mir in den Finger geschnitten.
– Bleib da! Ich finde ein Pflaster für dich.
4 – Kann ich Ihnen helfen? Was ist passiert?
– Ich bin ausgerutscht und hingefallen. Meine Hand tut mir schrecklich weh.
– Ich rufe sofort einen Arzt. Ich bin gleich wieder da.

5 – Oh! Mein Kopf tut weh!
– Was fehlt dir denn?
– Ich habe Kopfschmerzen! Es ist ganz schrecklich!
– Geh ins Bett! Ich bringe dir einige Tabletten.
6 – Mutti! Was ist los?
– Nichts Schlimmes. Ich habe mir nur gerade den Arm am Kochherd verbrannt.
– Komm. Du musst den Arm sofort mit kaltem Wasser kühlen. Ich helfe dir.
7 – Christian, was ist mit dir los?
– Ich bin vom Rad gefallen und mein Bein tut weh.
– Ist deine Mutti zu Hause?
– Ja.
– Bleib da! Ich hole sie für dich. Keine Angst haben!
8 – Mein Fuß! Mein Fuß!
– Was hast du denn?
– Ich bin auf einen Nagel getreten. Au … mein Fuß tut so weh …
– Setz dich hin und lass mich mal sehen!

Kontrolle 2: Sprechen

Page 60

This section consists of three speaking tests to measure students' understanding of a range of material covered in **Teil 2**.

1 Students provide responses for the dialogue set in a tourist information office using the picture cues.

2 Students respond to three questions from a waiter by selecting one response from the three picture cues.

3 Students respond to the girl's questions about their holiday, using the picture cues.

Kontrolle 3: Lesen

Page 61

This section consists of three reading tests to measure students' understanding of a range of material covered in **Teil 2**.

1 Students match the nine written descriptions to the illustrations by writing the appropriate letter in the box, as shown in the example.

2 Students read the postcard, then answer in English the four questions which follow.

3 Students read the letter and then decide whether the eight statements are true, false or not mentioned in the text.

Kontrolle 4: Schreiben

Page 62

This section consists of four writing tests to measure students' understanding of a range of material covered in **Teil 2**.

1 Students complete written reservations using the picture cues.

2 Students write a letter in German booking hotel accommodation, to include the information requested in the memo.

3 Students write a postcard in German in response to the questions, using the picture cues.

4 Students write a postcard in German in response to the questions.

TEIL 3

A Guten Appetit!

Page 4

1 Worträtsel: Was essen wir?

This wordsearch task may be used to consolidate key vocabulary from **exercise 1** on **p.86** of the main course-book.

- Students identify the food items in the wordsearch grid and write them out with the definite article.
- Students can check their own work in pairs, using a dictionary to check genders, before answers are fed back in a whole-class session.
- Follow-up: students construct their own wordsearches or crosswords. The best of these may be kept and used as a resource.

Page 5

2 Was isst du gern? Was trinkst du gern?

a This task serves as an easier alternative to **exercise 3a** on **p.86** of the main course-book.

- Brainstorm foods and drinks as a whole-class activity, writing up the results on the board/OHT.
- Students write out their favourite menu for each meal.
- Less able students restrict their choices to the list compiled on the board/OHT. More able students may use a dictionary to include other foods and drinks.

b This task serves as an easier alternative to **exercise 3a** on **p.86** of the main course-book. It provides oral consolidation of the vocabulary from task 2a above.

- Students question each other about their menus and note their partner's answers.
- Students check their own work in pairs, by comparing their notes with their partner's menu.
- Follow-up: students present their menus as café, restaurant or B&B menus, using DTP if possible and incorporating clip art or photos.

3 Geburtstagsfeier

This gap-fill task revises the past tenses in preparation for **exercise 4** on **p.87** of the main course-book.

- Preparation: revise the formation of the perfect tense (with auxiliary *haben* and *sein*) and the imperfect of *haben*.
- Students complete the past-tense sentences with the verb forms on the balloons.
- Remind less able students to cross off each verb form when it has been used.
- Check answers as a whole-class activity.
- Students write out a fair copy of the sentences.

Haushaltshilfe

Page 6

1 Wie hilfst du zu Hause?

a This matching task serves as an introduction or alternative to **exercise 1** on **p.88** of the main course-book.

- Preparation: check students' comprehension of the visuals and revise key verbs.
- Students read the sentences and select the matching visuals.
- Answers can be checked as a whole-class, group-work or pair-work activity.
- Follow-up: in a whole-class session, ask students what they do to help at home, in preparation for task 1b below.

b This oral pair-work task serves as an introduction or alternative to **exercises 1c** and **1d** on **p.88** of the main course-book.

- Working in pairs, students say what they do and how frequently, using the verbs from task 1a above and the words from the *Hilfe* box.
- Follow-up work: students write out the list of tasks they do to help at home.

Wir feiern!

Page 7

1 Wie feiert man?

a This matching task serves as an introduction to **exercise 1** on **p.90** of the main course-book.

- Students match the questions and answers.
- Students can check their own work in pairs by practising the dialogue.

b This is a written follow-up to task 1a above, and serves as an introduction or alternative to **exercise 3** on **p.90** of the main course-book.

- Preparation: go through the texts in **exercise 1** on **p.90** of the main course-book for relevant vocabulary.
- Students write sentences about their own favourite celebrations.
- Check students' work individually.

2 Pauls Geburtstag

This listening task serves as an introduction or alternative to **exercise 4** on **p.91** of the main course-book.

- Students listen to the recording and answer the questions. There is no need for them to write full sentences.
- Check answers as a whole-class activity.

> **Transcript:**
> Hallo, Richard! Hier spricht Paul. Wie geht's dir? Du, am 10. Oktober hatte ich Geburtstag! Ich habe bei mir zu Hause eine Party gemacht. Die Party hat um acht Uhr begonnen. Wir haben viel getanzt, gegessen und getrunken. Die Party war erst um Mitternacht zu Ende und hat viel Spaß gemacht. Meine Eltern haben die Party aber nicht so toll gefunden – für sie war das total langweilig. Wenn du Zeit hast, ruf mich an! Tschüs!

3 Unsere Party

This creative writing/speaking task provides an easier alternative to **exercise 7** on **p.91** of the main course-book, since a visual is provided as a stimulus for students' writing/speaking.

- Preparation: look at the visual with the whole class, asking questions in the perfect tense to elicit details:
  T: *Was hat man gegessen?* etc.
- Students write an account of the party. More able students can add their own imaginative details. Less able students can use their answers to task 2 above as a model.
- Check students' written work individually.
- Students make a recording based on their written work.
- Less able students may find it easier to do the recording as pair-work, asking each other questions based on those in task 2 above.

B Was isst du gern?

Page 8

Tasks 1 and 2 consolidate the vocabulary from **exercise 1a** on **p.92** of the main course-book and revise other common foods.

1 Astrid

- Students complete the crossword, using the picture clues.
- Less able students may use a dictionary.

2 Gabi

- Students complete the crossword, using the picture clues.
- Less able students may use a dictionary.

3 *Gern, nicht gern* oder *am liebsten*?

This writing task practises the key structures required for **exercises 1a–d** on **p.92** of the main course-book.

- Preparation: check students' understanding of the picture cues. Model the key structures by talking about your own food preferences:
  T: *Ich esse nicht gern Fisch*, etc.
- Students write sentences with *Ich esse gern/nicht gern/am liebsten …* , in response to the picture cues.
- Check answers as a whole-class activity.

Gesundheit und Fitness

Page 9

1 Was essen sie gern?

This listening task provides an introduction or easier alternative to **exercise 1** on **p.94** of the main course-book.

- Preparation: elicit from the class the German names of the foods and drinks shown in the pictures.
- Students listen to the recording and write down the number of each speaker next to the relevant picture.
- Check answers as a whole-class activity.
- Follow-up: play the recording again and ask students to listen out for adjectives relating to healthy eating:
  T: *Was sagen sie? Ist das gesund oder ungesund?*

TEIL 3

> **Transcript**
>
> 1 Ich esse viel Salat. Das ist langweilig, aber gesund!
> 2 Mein Lieblingsessen? Das ist Fastfood! Hamburger mit Pommes und viel Majo – lecker!
> 3 Ich trinke am liebsten Cola. Aber Diät-Cola trinke ich nicht. Igitt!
> 4 Ich trinke wahrscheinlich zu viel Kaffee. Vielleicht fünf oder sechs Tassen am Tag. Meine Mutter sagt immer, das ist ungesund!
> 5 Ich esse am liebsten Nudelgerichte. Dazu trinke ich viel Mineralwasser. Mineralwasser ist gesund.
> 6 Also, ich esse sehr gern Kuchen. Zum Beispiel Schokoladentorte. Ich weiß, ich weiß: Das macht dick. Aber Kuchen schmeckt total lecker!

2 Jetzt seid ihr dran!

This pair-work speaking task provides an introduction or easier alternative to **exercise 4** on **p.95** of the main coursebook.

- Preparation: revise subordinate clause word order after *weil*. Refer students to the *Hilfe* box on **p.95** of the main course-book.
- Students describe their preferences amongst the foods and drinks featured in task 1 above, giving reasons for their preferences using *weil*.

Lebst du gesund?

Page 10

1 Was machen sie?

This reading task provides an introduction to **exercise 1** on **p.96** of the main course-book.

- Preparation: examine the pictures with the class and elicit key words to describe each one.
- Students read the speech bubbles and find the two pictures which belong with each bubble.
- Follow-up: students use the pictures as cues for speaking practice:
  A: *Bild a und Bild f!*
  B: *Ich spiele gern Badminton und ich esse gern Schokolade*, etc.

2 Was hältst du von Sport?

This reading task will serve as an introduction or easier alternative to **exercise 2a** on **p.96** of the main course-book.

- Students read the statements and decide which are in favour of sport and which are against it.
- Students can check their answers in pairs.
- Follow-up: students make further statements dafür and dagegen. This could be made into a team game:
  Team A: *Dafür!*
  Team B: *Ich fahre gern Ski. Dagegen!*
  Team A: *Ich gehe lieber ins Kino. …* etc.

Page 11

3 Was tust du für deine Gesundheit?

This combined listening and reading task may be used as an easier alternative to **exercise 3** on **p.97** of the main course-book. It simplifies the task by separating it into two stages.

a This listening task uses a simplified version of the recording from the main course-book.
- Preparation: check comprehension of statements 1–9 before playing the recording.
- Students listen to the recording in sections. They then read the statements and decide which speaker they apply to.

> **Transcript**
>
> – Mein Name ist Björn. Morgens, also vor der Schule, esse ich nichts – ich habe zum Frühstücken keine Zeit. Und auf dem Weg zur Schule rauche ich eine oder zwei Zigaretten. Und nach der Schule zünde ich mir dann auch erstmal 'ne Zigarette an. Mittags essen wir vegetarisch – ich esse kein Fleisch, aber ich mag Gemüse.
> – Ich bin Golo, und ich will unbedingt dünn sein – ich bin viel zu dick! Ich trinke darum keinen Alkohol und ich esse jeden Tag nur einen Apfel und eine Scheibe Brot. Das ist manchmal ganz schön schwer und ich bin oft sehr müde – und Sport ist viel zu anstrengend für mich. Aber das ist mir egal!
> – Ich heiße Meike. Ich spiele Fußball im Verein und trainiere fast jeden Tag. Zum Essen habe ich nicht viel Zeit – ich esse mittags meist Hamburger und Pommes oder Currywurst. Das ist schnell und bequem. Am Wochenende gehe ich mit meinen Freunden in die Disco. Dort trinke ich dann immer einige Biere.

b This reading/discussion task is a follow-up to task 3a.

- Students decide which of the statements describe a healthy lifestyle and which ones describe an unhealthy lifestyle.

TEIL 3

- Check answers as a whole-class activity. There is scope for individual differences of opinion about some statements, which could be discussed or put to the vote.
- Follow-up: students write their own list of 'healthy' and 'unhealthy' statements. This could be made into a poster or web page.

4 Lebst du gesund – oder ungesund?

This guided oral pair-work task may be used as an introduction or easier alternative to **exercise 4** on **p.97** of the main course-book.

- Students make up their own dialogues with the help of the visual prompts provided. They can record their dialogues on tape.
- Follow-up: students make up further dialogues for real or imaginary people.

C Jobben

Page 12

1 Ich habe einen Job

This listening task may be used as an introduction or easier alternative to **exercise 1** on **p.98** of the main course-book.

- Students listen to the recording in two parts and choose the correct pictures for Kathi and Ina.

> **Transcript**
> – Ich heiße Kathi und ich bin 16 Jahre alt. Ich jobbe – ich arbeite als Zeitungsausträgerin. Also, ich arbeite jeden Mittwochnachmittag gleich nach der Schule. Ich trage 500 Zeitungen aus und das dauert ungefähr drei Stunden. Die Arbeit ist nicht besonders anstrengend und ich bekomme nicht viel Geld dafür: Ich verdiene 20 Euro pro Woche. Darum jobbe ich jetzt auch als Babysitterin. Da bekomme ich 8 Euro pro Stunde und die Arbeit ist nie langweilig – und ich mag Kinder.
> – Ich bin die Ina. Ich bin 18 Jahre alt und ich habe zwei Jobs. Ich jobbe am Wochenende in einem Café. Ich arbeite dort als Kellnerin. Ich bekomme 10 Euro pro Stunde. Die Arbeit ist ziemlich anstrengend – ich habe immer viel zu tun. Und in den Sommerferien arbeite ich in einer Autofabrik. Die Arbeit ist unheimlich langweilig, aber ich bekomme viel Geld dafür – ich bekomme 14 Euro pro Stunde. Und was ich mit dem ganzen Geld mache? Ich spare für einen Computer.

- Students listen again and note down any three additional details for each person they can, e.g. price, etc.

2 Jobben

a This writing task may be used as an introduction or easier alternative to **exercise 2a** on **p.98** of the main course-book.

- Preparation: revise *Ich arbeite/jobbe als/in …* and key vocabulary.
- Students write statements using the picture cues and the *Hilfe* box.

b This follow-up oral pair-work task may be used as an introduction or easier alternative to **exercise 2b** on **p.98** of the main course-book.

- Students ask each other about their jobs and answer as Tom, Nina, etc., using the picture cues and their answers to task 2a above.
- Follow-up: students record their dialogues.

Page 13

3 Ich suche einen Job

This listening task may be used for additional practice in conjunction with **exercise 3a** on **p.99** of the main course-book.

- Students listen to the recording and note down the key details for each job.
- Less able students are given the key details in scrambled order.
- Check answers as a whole-class activity.
- Follow-up: students work together in pairs to prepare and record their own versions of the dialogue, using different job details.

> **Transcript**
> – Jobvermittlung, guten Tag.
> – Ja, guten Tag. Mein Name ist Torben Mahler und ich suche einen Teilzeitjob.
> – So … Torben Mahler … Und wie alt sind Sie, Herr Mahler?
> – Ich bin 17.
> – Gut, das ist in Ordnung. Moment, ich schaue mal … ich habe einen Job als Verkäufer in einer Bäckerei …
> – Aha … und wann ist das?
> – Das ist einmal pro Woche – am Samstag.
> – Am Samstag – und wie lange … also, wie viele Stunden sind das?
> – Das ist von 9 Uhr bis 16 Uhr – sieben Stunden.
> – Und wie viel Geld?
> – Neun Euro pro Stunde.
> – Hmm … Haben Sie noch andere Jobs?

TEIL 3

> – Ja, ich habe auch noch einen Job als Zeitungsausträger.
> – Zeitungsausträger – und wann ist das?
> – Das ist jeden Mittwochnachmittag.
> – Und für wie viele Stunden?
> – Der Job ist von 15 Uhr bis 18 Uhr – das sind also drei Stunden.
> – Drei Stunden … Und wie viel Geld ist das?
> – Ääh, ich schaue mal. … Acht Euro pro Stunde.
> – Acht Euro?? So wenig? Okay, vielen Dank. Ich melde mich nächste Woche vielleicht wieder.
> – Alles klar, Herr Mahler. Auf Wiederhören!

4 Und wo arbeitest du?

a This multiple-choice task may be used as an introduction or easier alternative to **exercise 3** on **p.99** of the main course-book.

- Students read the letter and choose the correct answers.
- When checking answers, encourage students to identify the part of the text on which they based their answer.

b This guided writing task may be used as an introduction or easier alternative to **exercise 5** on **p.99** of the main course-book.

- Preparation: elicit oral answers for each question from the class.
- Students write a letter describing a job, in response to the prompts. The letter should be written on computer if possible, to facilitate the follow-up task.
- Follow-up: students adapt the letter to describe another job of their choice.

Arbeitspraktikum

Page 14

1 Das ideale Arbeitspraktikum

a This matching task reinforces the key vocabulary for **exercise 1** on **p.100** of the main coursebook.

- Students match up the phrases with the pictures.
- Check answers and comprehension as a whole-class activity.

b This follow-up pair-work task provides oral consolidation of the language from task 1a above. It provides an easier alternative to **exercise 1b** on **p.100** of the main course-book.

- Students take it in turns to choose their ideal work experience placement and give reasons for their choice, using phrases from task 1a.
- Follow-up: students record their dialogues on tape.

Page 15

2 Beim Berufsberater

a This listening task may be used as an introduction or easier alternative to **exercise 2** on **p.100** of the main course-book.

- Preparation: check comprehension of key vocabulary.
- Students listen to the recording in sections and correct the mistakes.
- Check answers as a whole-class activity.
- Follow-up: students ask each other for their personal details and write them down, in preparation for task 2b below.

> **Transcript**
> – So, du möchtest also ein Arbeitspraktikum machen?
> – Ja.
> – Und wann möchtest du das Praktikum machen?
> – In den Sommerferien.
> – Wie heißt du?
> – Jens Staade – S-T-A-A-D-E.
> – Wie alt bist du, Jens?
> – Ich bin 15 Jahre alt.
> – Und wo wohnst du?
> – Wasserweg 31.
> – Wie ist deine Telefonnummer?
> – 60 20 31.
> – Gut. So, Jens, was sind denn deine Lieblingsfächer?
> – Deutsch und Englisch.
> – Und welche Fächer magst du nicht so gern?
> – Informatik. Informatik mag ich gar nicht.
> – Und welche Interessen hast du?
> – Also, ich interessiere mich sehr für Umweltschutz.
> – Aha … Jens, und was meinst du – was für ein Mensch bist du?
> – Na ja, ich bin sehr kontaktfreudig. Ich arbeite gern mit anderen Menschen zusammen.
> – Gut, das ist alles, Jens.

b This task provides written consolidation of task 2a above.

- Students fill in the form with their own personal information.

TEIL 3

3 Schüler für Praktikum gesucht!

This task may be used as an introduction or easier alternative to **exercise 4b** on **p.101** of the main course-book.

- Students read the statements and compare them with the advertisements on **p.161** of the main course-book.
- Students decide whether the statements are true, false or not in the text.
- Follow-up: students correct any false statements.

Wie war dein Praktikum?

Page 16

1 Wie war es?

This matching task reinforces key adjectives for use with **exercises 4** and **5** on **p.103** in the main course-book.

- Students match the pictures with the words.

2 Hat dir die Arbeit gefallen?

a This listening task may be used as an introduction or easier alternative to **exercise 4** on **p.103** of the main course-book.

- Preparation: check comprehension of key vocabulary.
- Students listen to the recording and match up the sentence halves.
- More able students match up the sentence halves before listening to the recording.
- Follow-up: as a pair-work task, students question each other about summer/weekend jobs they have done.

> **Transcript**
> – Silke, wo hast du dein Praktikum gemacht?
> – Ich habe vier Wochen in einer Gärtnerei gearbeitet.
> – Aha ... Und wie hat dir die Arbeit gefallen?
> – Also, das Praktikum war sehr interessant und die Arbeit hat mir sehr gut gefallen. Ich konnte selbstständig arbeiten – das war auch toll.
> – Und was hat dir sonst noch gefallen?
> – Es war nie langweilig. Und ich habe viel gelernt. Das war auch super.
> – Und was hat dir nicht gefallen?
> – Das Wetter! Das Wetter war sehr schlecht. Es hat fast jeden Tag geregnet und es war kalt. Und die Arbeit war auch ziemlich anstrengend.

b This follow-up task provides written consolidation of the language from task 2a above.

- Students write a few sentences describing Silke's work experience using the language from task 2a.

3 Hat dir das Praktikum gefallen?

This oral pair-work task may be used as an introduction or easier alternative to **exercise 5b** on **p.103** of the main course-book.

- Students make up their own dialogues with the help of the picture cues.
- Follow-up: students record their dialogues on tape.

D Wir gehen aus!

Page 17

1 Kreuzworträtsel

This crossword be used as an introduction or follow-up task to **exercise 3** on **p.108** of the main course-book.

- Students complete the clue sentences using the pictures, and fill in the crossword.
- Follow-up: more able students devise their own crosswords. The best examples can be kept and used as a resource.

2 Hast du Lust ... ?

This oral pair-work task is a more structured alternative to **exercise 3** on **p.108** of the main course-book. It revises the structures featured in the *Hilfe* box on **p.108** of the main course-book.

- Preparation: go through the examples with the whole class. Check comprehension of the other symbols used in the task.
- Students take it in turns to suggest outings and respond according to the picture cues.
- Follow-up: students improvise their own dialogues.

Page 18

3 Wann und wo treffen sie sich?

This listening task can be used as preparation for **exercise 3** on **p.108** of the main course-book.

- Preparation: revise the places around town and the clock times shown.

35

TEIL 3

- Students listen to the recording and tick the symbols which correspond to the arrangements made (place and time). The task may be completed in two stages.
- Check answers as a whole-class activity.
- Follow-up: students use their completed answers as the basis for simple written dialogues, before going on to **exercise 3** on **p.108** of the main course-book.

Transcript

1 – Also. Wo treffen wir uns heute Abend?
  – An der Bushaltestelle.
  – Gut. Und wann treffen wir uns?
  – Um halb sieben.
  – An der Bushaltestelle um halb sieben. Abgemacht!
2 – Wo treffen wir uns denn? Am Theater?
  – Ja, am Theater.
  – Und die Vorstellung beginnt um acht Uhr. Also, wann treffen wir uns, meinst du?
  – Um Viertel vor acht.
  – Schön. Wir sehen uns am Theater um Viertel vor acht. Bis später!
3 – Möchtest du heute Abend … vielleicht … mit mir ausgehen?
  – Ja. Gern!
  – Toll! Wo treffen wir uns?
  – Am Café?
  – Ja. Am Café wäre schön. Und wann?
  – Um sieben Uhr?
  – Ja. Am Café um sieben Uhr. Ich freue mich!
  – Ich auch …
4 – Gut! Hast du alles kapiert?
  – Ja … Ich … denke schon.
  – Also. Dann sag mir: Wo treffen wir uns?
  – An der Schule.
  – Und wann treffen wir uns?
  – Um 20 vor sieben.
  – Toll. An der Schule um 20 vor sieben. Bitte nicht vergessen!
5 – Haben Sie schon die Pläne für heute Abend? Wo treffen wir uns? Und wann?
  – Nicht so laut, bitte! Nun, hören Sie gut zu. Wir treffen uns am Marktplatz um 10 nach fünf. Wiederholen Sie, bitte!
  – Am Marktplatz um fünf nach 10.
  – Nein! Nein! Um 10 nach fünf. Verstanden?
  – Wir treffen uns am Marktplatz um 10 nach fünf. Verstanden.
  – Na, gut. Bis heute Abend.
6 – Kommst du heute mit zum Hallenbad?
  – Ja, sicher. Wo treffen wir uns?
  – Am Hallenbad. Um 10 vor vier.
  – Am Hallenbad um 10 vor vier. Gut. Aber ich muss zuerst Mutti Bescheid sagen.
  – Ja, klar.
  – Tschüs!
  – Tschüs. Bis später!

Page 19

4 Kommst du zu meiner Party?

a This listening task may be used as an introduction or easier alternative to **exercise 5** on **p.109** of the main course-book.

- Students listen to the recording in sections and find the correct pictures.
- Check answers as a whole-class activity.

Transcript

1 – Dohrmann!
  – Hallo, Sven, hier ist Anna.
  – Hallo, Anna!
  – Du, Sven, hast du am Samstag Zeit? Ich habe Geburtstag und möchte dich gern zu meiner Party einladen.
  – Eine Geburtstagsparty – super! Vielen Dank für die Einladung! Ja, ich komme gern. Wann beginnt die Party?
  – So, um 19 Uhr. Also, bis Samstag dann! Tschüs!
  – Ja, bis Samstag!
2 – Mareike Klar.
  – Hallo, Mareike, ich bin's – Svenja.
  – Hi, Svenja!
  – Mareike, ich mache am Samstag eine Party – eine Faschingsparty. Möchtest du zu meiner Party kommen?
  – Ja, gern – vielen Dank für die Einladung. Soll ich etwas mitbringen? Etwas zu essen oder Getränke?
  – Nein, das brauchst du nicht. Es gibt Salate und Kuchen.
  – Gut. Also, nochmals vielen Dank für die Einladung. Wir sehen uns dann am Samstag!
3 – Meier.
  – Hallo, Ina, hier ist Andi.
  – Hallo, Andi, wie geht's?
  – Gut, danke. Ina, hast du am Samstag schon was vor?
  – Nein, warum?
  – Mein Austauschpartner Ben fährt am Sonntag wieder nach England zurück. Ich mache eine Abschiedsparty für ihn. Kommst du zu meiner Party?
  – Ja klar, ich komme gern. Wo ist die Party? Bei dir zu Hause?
  – Ja, die Party ist in unserem Partykeller. Sie beginnt um 20 Uhr.
  – Super, bis Samstag dann! Und nochmals vielen Dank für die Einladung!

b This pair-work task provides guided oral practice of the language from task 4a.

- Students invite each other to the parties from task 4a with the help of the phrases from the *Hilfe* box.

Page 20

5 Maria macht eine Party

a This matching task may be used as an introduction to **exercise 6** on **p.109** of the main course-book.

- Students match the speech bubbles to the appropriate cartoons.

b This oral pair-work task is a follow-up to task 5a.

- Students make up their own simple dialogues using the sentences from task 5a above.
- Students record their dialogues on tape.
- Extension: more able students adapt the model sentences given, e.g. *Ich muss auf meinen Bruder aufpassen*, or make up their own reasons. Less able students can also attempt this, but should be provided with suggestions.

Unterhaltung und Kultur

Page 21

1 Fernsehsendungen

a This wordsearch provides some basic revision of television programme types, as well as reinforcing the need for accuracy of spelling. It serves as an introduction to **exercise 1** on **p.112** of the main course-book.

- Preparation: brainstorm programme types with the class.
- Preparation: check that students understand the different types by naming various programmes and asking in German what category they belong to.
- Students ring the words in the wordsearch grid and then copy them out.
- Check the answers as a whole-class activity. Draw the wordsearch on the board or an OHT, then ring the words according to the class's instructions.
- Follow-up: students create their own wordsearches or alternatively crosswords using symbols or English/German clues. The best wordsearches/crosswords could be copied and used as a resource.

b This is a written follow-up to task 1a

- Students write down the English translations of the programme types.
- Less able students can be provided with the translations in jumbled order.

2 Was gab es gestern im Fernsehen?

This writing task serves as an introduction or alternative to **exercise 2** on **p.112** of the main course-book. Teachers need to be aware that on religious and moral grounds some students may not be allowed to watch all TV programmes, and some may not be able to watch any. In this case, the task should be adapted to a reduced list of programmes or a list of radio programmes.

- Preparation: provide copies of TV guides, either from TV listings magazines or websites.
- Students select a number of programmes and write out the titles. They then categorise the programmes and write short comments next to them. More able students should be encouraged to write full sentences and give more detail.
- Students can use word-processing, DTP or web-design software to give their comments a 'professional' presentation, as critiques from a TV listings magazine or a website.

3 Kritik

This writing task is a more structured alternative to **exercise 4** on **p.113** of the main course-book.

- Preparation: revise *weil* and subordinate clause word order. Go through the vocabulary and structures in the *Hilfe* box on **p.113** of the main course-book.
- Students answer three questions to write a short critique of a book, film, concert, radio programme or TV programme.
- Students can use word-processing, DTP or web-design software to give their critiques a 'professional' presentation, as critiques from a TV listings magazine or a website.

E Taschengeld und Einkaufen

Page 22

1 Wer sagt was?

This matching task reinforces the key vocabulary in the *Hilfe* box on **p.114** of the main course-book.

- Students match the pictures to the speech bubbles.

TEIL 3

- Follow-up: ask students who gets pocket money, how much and what they spend it on.
- Less able students might prefer to conduct a survey and present the results.

2 Bekommst du Taschengeld?

This listening task may be used as an introduction or easier alternative to **exercise 1** on **p.114** of the main course-book.

- Preparation: check comprehension of the visuals.
- Students listen to the recording and complete the grid for Nele and Felix.
- Check answers as a whole-class activity.
- Follow-up: students ask each other about pocket money: *Bekommst du Taschengeld? Wie viel? Was kaufst du davon? Sparst du etwas?*

Transcript

– Nele, bekommst du Taschengeld?
– Ja, ich bekomme jeden Monat 60 Euro.
– Und kommst du mit deinem Taschengeld aus?
– O nein, ich komme damit nicht aus.
– Und was kaufst du alles von deinem Taschengeld?
– Ich muss von meinem Taschengeld alles kaufen: Schulsachen, modische Klamotten … Na ja, und dann kaufe ich mir jede Woche noch Jugendzeitschriften und am Wochenende gehe ich in die Disco.
– Und sparst du auch etwas von deinem Taschengeld?
– Nein, das kann ich nicht! Ich gebe alles aus.

– Bekommst du Taschengeld, Felix?
– Ja, ich bekomme jede Woche 20 Euro.
– Du bekommst also pro Monat 80 Euro. Und das ist genug? Kommst du damit aus?
– Ja, ich komme damit aus. Ich habe auch keine teuren Hobbys und so …
– Wofür gibst du dein Taschengeld denn aus?
– Für Computerzeitschriften. Und manchmal gehe ich mit meinem Freund ins Kino.
– Und wie ist das mit Sachen für die Schule und mit Kleidung?
– Das kauft alles meine Mutter.
– Und sparst du auch etwas von deinem Taschengeld?
– Ja, ich spare jeden Monat 7 Euro.

3 Taschengeld

This multiple-choice reading task may be used as an introduction or easier alternative to **exercise 4** on **p.114** of the main course-book.

- Students read the letter and choose the correct answers.
- Check answers as a whole-class activity, with students justifying their answers with reference to the text.

Page 23

4 Internetshopping vs. Stadtmitte

a This reading task uses key vocabulary from **exercise 5** on **p.115** of the main course-book. It can be completed either as a whole-class discussion activity to introduce exercise 5, or individually as a follow-up.

- As an introduction: present the phrases in the box on the board/an OHT and check comprehension, e.g. by miming, drawing sketches or paraphrasing and asking students to select the appropriate phrase.
- Ask the class to categorise each phrase: T: *Viel Stress: hat man das in der Stadtmitte?* etc. Students may decide that some phrases relate to both kinds of shopping.
- As a follow-up: students complete the task individually or in pairs, referring back to their notes for **exercise 5b** on **p.115** of the main course-book as necessary.
- Check answers as a whole-class activity. Students may decide that some phrases relate to both kinds of shopping.

b This task is a follow-up to task 4a above and also an introduction or easier alternative to **exercise 6** on **p.115** of the main course-book.

- Students categorise the phrases from task 4a as advantages or disadvantages. Note that there is scope for differing opinions in their answers.

Im Supermarkt

Page 24

1 Im Supermarkt: Ein Worträtsel

This anagram task concentrates just on quantities and as such will serve as a simple introduction to **exercise 2** on **p.116** of the main course-book.

- Students unjumble the quantity words using **exercise 2** on **p.116** of the main course-book for reference.

TEIL 3

2 Was darf es sein?

This gap-fill task will serve as an introduction to **exercise 3** on **p.116** of the main course-book and again concentrates on quantities, this time combined with the food and in full sentences.

- Students work individually or in pairs to fill in the gaps, using words from the box.
- Check answers as a whole-class activity.
- Follow-up: students write a fair copy of the sentences.

3 Das Picknick

This writing/role-play shopping task will serve as a simpler version of **exercise 5** on **p.117** of the main course-book, or as a supplement to it.

a This is the writing element of the task.

- Preparation: revise the names of the items illustrated. This may be written on the board for weaker students to copy.
- Students might suggest additions.
- Students write a shopping list in German based on the illustrations.

b This is the oral pair-work element of the task.

- Students work in pairs to practise a dialogue based on the shopping list in task 3a.
- The dialogues may be recorded on tape.

Im Kaufhaus

Page 25

1 Wo finde ich … ?

a This matching task introduces the key vocabulary for **exercises 1** and **2** on **p.118** of the main course-book.

- Students match up the pictures with the information from the store directory and label the different departments.
- Less able students reinforce their work by writing out the store guide in the correct sequence.
- Check answers as a whole-class activity.
- Follow-up: for homework students write out a German guide to their local/favourite store.

b This listening task may be used as a follow-up to **exercise 1** on **p.118** of the main course-book.

- Students listen to the recording in sections and note Herr Huber's answers.

- Students compare Herr Huber's answers with the store plan from task 1a and correct his mistakes.
- Check answers as a whole-class activity.

Transcript
– Entschuldigung!
– Ähh … Ja bitte?
– Bücher – wo finde ich Bücher?
– Bücher … Bücher sind … im ersten Stock.
– Und wo ist der Computer-Shop?
– Hmm … der Computer-Shop, ja, also, der Computer-Shop befindet sich im … ersten Stock.
– Vielen Dank.
– Entschuldigen Sie bitte! Ich suche Kinderkleidung.
– Aha … ja.
– Also, wo finde ich Kinderkleidung?
– Moment … Kinderkleidung – Kinderkleidung ist … im Keller!
– Danke. Und wo ist die Musikabteilung?
– Die … die Musikabteilung? Also, die Musikabteilung befindet sich … im Erdgeschoss.
– Entschuldigung!
– J-j-ja?
– Sagen Sie, wo finde ich Schreibwaren?
– Ja … Moment … Schreibwaren, Schreibwaren, Schreibwaren … sind im … im ersten Stock.
– Im ersten Stock. Und wo sind Zeitschriften?
– Zeitschriften?? Also, Zeitschriften befinden sich … befinden sich …
– Ja, wo??
– Zeitschriften befinden sich im zweiten Stock, ja, im zweiten Stock.
– Und wo sind … ? Hallo? Bleiben Sie hier!! Hallo!!

c In this oral pair-work task, students use the information from task 1b and the *Hilfe* box to make up dialogues with the correct answers about the department store.

Page 26

2 Worträtsel

This task revises key clothing vocabulary in preparation for **exercises 3–5** on **pp.118–19** of the main course-book.

a Students find eight items of clothing in the grid.

b Students match up the words from task 1a with the pictures.

c Students make up their own dialogues using the nouns from task 1a.

TEIL 3

- Follow-up: students devise their own wordsearches for different items of clothing, departments, etc.

3 Was kostet das?

This matching task revises prices and numbers.

- Students match up the price tags with the amounts written out in full.
- Follow-up: provide less able students with further practice on the board/an OHT, or as a bingo game, etc.

Page 27

4 Was kaufen sie?

This listening task may be used as an introduction or easier alternative to **exercises 3** and **4** on **p.118** of the main course-book.

- Students listen to the recordings of Susi and Jan and complete the grid.
- Check answers as a whole-class activity.
- Follow-up: students add details of size and prices after additional hearings.

Transcript

Susi
– Guten Tag! Kann ich Ihnen helfen?
– Ja, ich suche Klamotten für den Sommer.
– Gern. Hier sind Blusen …
– Oh, diese Blusen sind schön.
– Welche Größe haben Sie?
– Größe 38.
– Hier, bitte. Die Umkleidekabinen sind dort drüben. … Passt die Bluse?
– Nein, die Bluse ist zu klein. Aber dieser Pullover gefällt mir. Was kostet der?
– Dieser Pullover kostet 29 Euro.
– Gut! Ich nehme ihn!

Jan
– Ja, bitte? Kann ich Ihnen helfen?
– Ja, ich suche Klamotten.
– Also, hier haben wir Hosen …
– Ja, diese Hose gefällt mir. Kann ich sie anprobieren?
– Ja, dort drüben.
– Nein, die Hose passt mir nicht. Schade. Hmm … und wo finde ich Hemden?
– Hier links. Hier – gefällt Ihnen dieses Hemd?
– O ja. Was kostet das Hemd?
– Es kostet 49 Euro.
– O nein – das ist mir zu teuer! Haben Sie etwas Billigeres?
– Also, wir haben T-Shirts im Angebot.
– T-Shirts? O ja, gut, ich nehme ein gestreiftes T-Shirt in Größe L.

2 Techno-Tom probiert Klamotten an – aber nichts passt!

This matching task revises key vocabulary as an alternative or supplement to exercise **6a** on **p.119** of the main course-book.

- Students match up the pictures with the speech bubbles.
- Follow-up: students enact role-plays based on the sentences and record them on tape.

Kontrolle 1: Hören

Page 28

This section consists of three listening tests to measure students' understanding of a range of material covered in **Teil 3**.

1 Students listen to the dialogue and decide who bought each item depicted.

Transcript

– Also, Anna, wonach schauen wir zuerst?
– Ich suche ein Kleid für die Party am Samstag! Und du, Bernd?
– Tja, ich suche eine Hose – am liebsten in Braun.
– Hier, schau mal, Bernd – Sonderangebote! Mensch, die Pullover hier sind im Angebot – total billig! Also, ich kaufe den Pullover in Weiß!
– Ja, und ich nehme das bunte T-Shirt – das passt mir bestimmt! Okay, und was suchst du noch, Anna?
– Eine Bluse – hier, diese Bluse gefällt mir! Wo sind die Umkleidekabinen? … Die Bluse passt. Ist das alles, Bernd?
– Nein, ich suche noch Turnschuhe von Adidas oder Puma – hoffentlich sind sie nicht zu teuer! … Ja, schau mal! Ganz billig! Die nehme ich auch!

2 Students listen to the dialogue and match the items to the visuals.

Transcript

– Peter! Kannst du bitte für mich einkaufen gehen?
– O.K. … Was muss ich denn kaufen?
– Nur ein paar Sachen.
– Was denn? Komm, ich schreibe eine Liste.
– Zwei Dosen Orangensaft, ein Kilo Karotten, eine Flasche Mineralwasser, eine Tüte Chips, eine Packung Reis, eine Tafel Schokolade und zweihundert Gramm Schinken.
– Ist das alles?!
– Nein … und zwei Flaschen Bier. Danke!

3 Students listen to the three answerphone messages and note down the information.

> **Transcript**
> – Hallo, Anja, ich bin's – Sven. Du, hast du heute Abend schon was vor? Ich gehe mit Meike ins Kino – im Scala gibt es den neuen Film mit Sylvester Stallone. Wir treffen uns um 20 Uhr am Bahnhof. Tschüs!
> – Anja? Hier ist Lena. Hast du heute Abend Zeit? Ich gehe mit meinem Bruder ins Café im Jugendzentrum. Und stell dir vor: Heiko aus der 10 B kommt auch mit!! Ja!!! Also, bis um 18 Uhr – ich hole dich zu Hause ab! Bis dann!
> – Anja, hallo, hier ist – also, hier ist der Rainer aus der 8 A. Ich habe heute Geburtstag und ich – ja, ich mache heute Abend eine Party ... und ich ... ähmm, also, ich möchte dich gern zu meiner Party einladen. Die Party ist bei mir zu Hause und beginnt um 19 Uhr 30.

Kontrolle 2: Sprechen

Pages 29–30

This section is a list of suggestions for topics for oral presentations, taken from the topics covered in **Teil 3**. For each topic, a range of questions is given. Students should use these questions as a guide in preparing their presentations, but should record their presentations as a continuous text, not as question and answer.

Kontrolle 3: Lesen

Page 31

This section consists of three reading tests to measure students' understanding of a range of material covered in **Teil 3**.

1 Students match the six written items on the shopping list to the appropriate departments on the store guide.

2 Students match the six written descriptions 1–6 to the six illustrations a–f.

3 Students read the letter and answer the six comprehension questions. It is not necessary for students to answer in full sentences.

Kontrolle 4: Schreiben

Page 32

This section consists of three writing tests to measure students' understanding of a range of material covered in **Teil 3**.

1 Students fill in the questionnaire on pocket money with their own details. It is not necessary for students to answer in full sentences.

2 Students write a card giving an excuse for not going to a party.

3 Students write a letter of application for a part-time job.

TEIL 4

A Wie bin ich?

Page 34

1 Das bin ich!

This matching task reinforces some key vocabulary for this topic.

- Preparation: practise the key vocabulary orally.
- Students match the speech bubbles to the pictures.
- Check answers as a whole-class activity.

2 Wir suchen Brieffreunde

This writing task may be used as an easier alternative to **exercise 1b** on **p.126** of the main course-book.

- Students fill in the identity card with their own personal details.
- Follow-up: students fill in the identity card for friends/family members/pop stars, etc.

3 Antwortbrief

This task consists of a gap-fill followed by a guided writing task. It provides students with the necessary framework for writing a letter describing themselves, and may be used as an introduction or easier alternative to **exercise 4** on **p.127** of the main course-book.

a Students read the letter and fill in the missing words.

b Students write a letter about themselves, using the previous task as a model. They could create a fictitious persona for themselves, or write in the person of a celebrity, film character etc.

Probleme

Page 35

1 Ich habe immer Streit mit meinen Eltern!

This listening task revises some key vocabulary for this topic.

- Preparation: look at the pictures with the class and encourage them to speculate about the nature of the problem:
  T: *Bild a – was ist das Problem? Was meint ihr?*
- Students listen to the recording and identify the correct pictures for the five speakers.
- Follow-up: students listen again to the recording and make brief notes about the nature of each problem.

Transcript

– Ich heiße Kathi. Meine Eltern sagen immer: „Du siehst zu viel fern – und immer Seifenopern!" Aber ich finde Fernsehen super! Das ist doch kein Problem, oder?
– Mein Name ist Annika und das Problem ist mein Zimmer. Ich bin nicht sehr ordentlich und meine Mutter findet das furchtbar.
– Ich heiße Uwe und habe Probleme mit meinen Eltern. Sie sind viel zu streng! Ich darf abends nur bis acht Uhr ausgehen.
– Ich bin die Katja und ich habe oft Streit mit meinen Eltern. Sie sagen immer: „Du hilfst nicht genug im Haushalt!" Aber ich wasche manchmal ab.
– Mein Name ist Philipp und das Problem ist die Schule. Ich finde Schule langweilig und ich habe ziemlich schlechte Noten. Ich streite mich deshalb oft mit meinen Eltern.

2 Geschwister

This multiple-choice listening task may be used as an introduction or easier alternative to **exercise 1** on **p.128** of the main course-book.

- Students listen to the recording and choose the correct ending for each sentence.
- Check answers as a whole-class activity.

Transcript

A Ich bin der Heiko. Ich bin 16 und habe zwei Geschwister – Anna ist 13 Jahre alt und Maximilian ist 14. Ich verstehe mich mit meinen Geschwistern ganz gut. Klar, ich habe manchmal Streit mit ihnen, zum Beispiel wegen der Hausarbeit, aber ich komme eigentlich gut mit Anna und Maximilian aus. Mit meinen Eltern ist das leider anders! Ich habe oft Probleme mit meinen Eltern – sie sind viel zu streng, finde ich.

B Ich heiße Silke und ich bin 15 Jahre alt. Ich habe zwei Schwestern – Laura ist 11 und Miriam ist 16. Wie wir uns verstehen? Ich verstehe mich mit meinen Eltern super, aber ich komme nicht so gut mit meinen Schwestern aus. Ich habe ab und zu Streit mit Miriam, aber am schlimmsten ist es mit Laura: Ich streite mich immer mit Laura! Sie ist viel zu frech und launisch und sie weint immer!

Page 36

3 Probleme mit den Eltern

This listening task may be used as an introduction or easier alternative to **exercise 3** on **p.129** of the main course-book.

- Preparation: students read the statements from the grid. Help them with any comprehension difficulties.
- Students listen to the recording in three sections and fill in the grid. They listen to each section as often as necessary.
- Help less able students by telling them to listen for two problems per person.
- Check answers as a whole-class activity.

> **Transcript**
> – Tina, verstehst du dich gut mit deinen Eltern?
> – Nein, meine Eltern sind total streng – das ist ein Problem.
> – Hast du oft Streit mit deinen Eltern?
> – Ja, sehr oft. Ich muss zum Beispiel abends schon um halb zehn zu Hause sein – und am Wochenende darf ich nur bis 11 Uhr ausgehen.
>
> – Marie, hast du Probleme mit deinen Eltern?
> – Ja, mit meinen Klamotten. Meine Mutter mag meine Klamotten nicht! Ich streite sehr oft mit meiner Mutter darüber. Und ich soll immer mein Zimmer aufräumen, aber ich mag eben Unordnung – und es ist doch mein Zimmer!
>
> – Frieder, hast du auch Probleme mit deinen Eltern?
> – Ja, mit der Schule. Meine Eltern sagen, ich bin zu faul. Aber das stimmt nicht. Und schlechte Noten sind auch ein Problem. Ja, deshalb habe ich oft Streit mit meinem Vater.

4 Leserbriefe

This task may be used as an introduction or easier alternative to **exercise 5** on **p.129** of the main course-book.

a Students read the letters 1–3 and match them up with the correct headings a–b.

b Students read the answers and match them up with the letters in 4a above.

- As a follow-up task, more able students could write their own problem letters based on a letter of their choice.

Freundschaft und Heirat

Page 37

1 Guter Freund, gute Freundin

This word puzzle revises key vocabulary for discussing personality and will serve as an introduction to **exercise 1** on **p.130** of the main coursebook.

- Students translate the adjectives into German and complete the word puzzle.
- Follow-up: more able students can research further personality adjectives with the help of a dictionary.

Page 38

2 Mein bester Freund

This gap-fill reading comprehension may be used as an introduction or easier alternative to **exercise 3** on **p.130** of the main course-book.

- Preparation: study the illustration with the class and elicit words to describe the two boys.
- Preparation: read the letter with the class. Establish whether each gap is likely to be a noun, a verb form or an adjective/adverb.
- Students work individually or in pairs to complete the letter with the words from the box.
- Check answers as a whole-class activity.
- Students write out a fair copy of the letter.
- Follow-up: students can use the letter as a model for a letter about their best friend, real or fictitious. They could write in the person of a celebrity or a fictional character from a book or film, etc.

3 Feste Freundschaften

This listening task may be used as an introduction or easier alternative to **exercise 5** on **p.131** of the main course-book.

- Preparation: check students' comprehension of the statements in the grid.
- Students listen to the recording several times, and decide whether each of the statements in the grid is true, false or not mentioned in the text.
- Check answers as a whole-class activity. Discuss any wrong answers. In particular, the difference between false answers and those not supported by the text is often difficult for students to grasp.

TEIL 4

Transcript

– Frauke, hast du einen festen Freund?
– Ja. Er heißt Adrian.
– Seit wann seid ihr zusammen?
– Also, wir sind seit sechs Monaten „zusammen", aber wir kennen uns seit sechs oder sieben Jahren.
– Und was macht ihr so zusammen?
– Tja, ganz normale Sachen ... wir gehen zusammen in die Disco, ins Kino und so. Aber wir verbringen auch viel Zeit bei mir zu Hause. Wir sitzen dann meistens in meinem Zimmer und lesen – wir sind furchtbar langweilig! Adrian versteht sich super mit meinen Eltern, was wirklich toll ist.
– Was ist das Wichtigste an einer festen Freundschaft?
– Also, ich finde, es ist total wichtig, dass man sich auf den Freund verlassen kann – er muss zuverlässig und treu sein.
– Aha. Was sind die Vorteile einer festen Freundschaft?
– Na, dass man alles miteinander besprechen kann, über alles reden kann.
– Und was sind die Nachteile?
– Schwierige Frage! Also ... vielleicht, dass man zu wenig Zeit mit seinen anderen Freundinnen oder Freunden verbringt.
– Frauke, danke für dieses Interview.

B Wo ich wohne

Page 39

1 Meine Heimatstadt

This listening task will serve as an introduction or easier alternative to **exercise 1** on **p.132** of the main course-book.

- Preparation: study the pictures in the workbook with the class and elicit a word to describe each picture.
- Students listen to the recording and select the pictures which answer the questions in the workbook about Karl's home town.
- Check answers as a whole-class activity.

Transcript

Ich wohne in einem Hochhaus in Rostock. Ich wohne gern dort. Wir haben natürlich keinen Garten, aber es gibt einen großen Park in der Nähe. Mein Vater arbeitet in einem Büro in der Stadtmitte und meine Mutter arbeitet nachmittags in einer Fabrik. Wir haben viele Fahrradwege in unserer Stadt und ich fahre jeden Tag mit dem Rad zur Schule. Es gibt viel Verkehr in unserer Stadt, aber es gibt auch eine große Fußgängerzone in der Stadtmitte.

2 In meiner Stadt ...

This sequencing task gives students an opportunity to revise word order as well as basic vocabulary relevant to the topic. It will serve as an introduction to task 3 below.

- Students put the words in the correct order to make sentences.
- Follow-up: students work in pairs to write and scramble sentences of their own (or from **exercise 1a** on **p.132** of the course-book) and present them to their partners to unscramble.

3 Ein Brief

This guided writing task provides a more structured alternative to **exercise 3** on **p.133** of the main course-book.

- Preparation: draw students' attention to the *Hilfe* box on **p.133** of the main course-book.
- Students write a letter of approximately 70 words in response to the questions.

Unsere Umwelt

Page 40

1 Umweltprobleme

This matching task may be used as an introduction or easier alternative to **exercise 1** on **p.134** of the main course-book.

- Preparation: study the four pictures with the class and elicit words to describe each one.
- Students match the sentences to the pictures.
- Check answers as a whole-class activity. Help students to find the meanings of the more advanced items of vocabulary in a dictionary.

2 Wie sollte man die Umwelt schützen?

This task is a follow-up to task 1 above.

- Students match the problems from task 1 to the solutions.

3 Du bist dran

This task is an easier alternative to **exercise 4a** on **p.135** of the main course-book.

TEIL 4

- Preparation: revise the structure *man muss/sollte* + infinitive, and draw students' attention to the *Hilfe* box on **p.135** of the main course-book.
- Students write four sentences recommending measures to protect the environment. They may, but need not, use the pictures in the workbook as prompts.
- Follow-up: students work together in small groups to develop further recommendations. They use ICT to present these in the form of a poster or web page.

Umweltschutz

Page 41

1 Was machen sie für die Umwelt?

This matching task provides basic reading material on the theme of the environment. It will serve as an introduction to **pp.136–137** of the main course-book.

a Students match up the pictures with the statements.

b Students decide which of the statements from task 1a are environmentally friendly and which ones are environmentally unfriendly.

Page 42

2 Das Umwelt-Quiz

Students test their knowledge of protecting the environment with this multiple-choice quiz.

- Preparation: check comprehension orally.
- Students complete the quiz individually or in pairs.
- Provide the answers on the board/OHT. Students work in pairs to check each other's answers.
- Follow-up: students create their own quiz.

C Welche Schule?

Page 43

1 In welche Schule gehen sie?

This matching task consolidates students' knowledge of the German school system. It should not be attempted until students have completed **exercises** 1 and 2 on **p.138** of the main course-book.

- Students select the school type which matches each statement.
- Check answers as a whole-class activity and go through any incorrect answers with the students.

2 Schule in Deutschland

This quiz tests students' knowledge of the German school system, and should not be attempted until students have completed **pp.138–39** of the main course-book.

- Students complete the quiz individually, in pairs or in small groups.
- Provide the correct answers on the board/OHT. Students hand over their answers to another student/pair/group to check.
- Follow-up: students create their own quiz in German about UK schools.

Deine Meinung

Page 44

1 Schuluniformen

This task may be used as an introduction or easier alternative to **exercise 1** on **p.140** of the main course-book.

a This reading task revises key adjectives for task 1b below.

- Students read the adjectives and decide which ones are positive and which are negative descriptions of school uniforms.
- Follow-up: students think up further adjectives to describe school uniforms.

b This writing task gives students the opportunity to express their own opinions without using *weil* + subordinate word order.

- Students give their own opinions on school uniforms in writing or orally using the adjectives from task 1a. This could also be set as a homework task.

2 Schulordnung

This gap-fill task may be used as an introduction to **exercise 2** on **pp.140–41** of the main course-book.

- Students complete the school rules using the words from the box.
- Check answers as a whole-class activity.
- Students write out a fair copy of the rules.

TEIL 4

- Follow-up: students write their own ideal school rules, e.g. *Man darf im Unterricht essen und trinken*, etc.

3 Ich würde …

This writing task may be used as an alternative to **exercise 6** on **p.141** of the main course-book.

- Preparation: revise the structure *ich würde* + infinitive.
- Refer students to the *Hilfe* box on **p.141** of the main course-book.
- Students write their own suggestions for improvements to their school. These could be illustrated with photos or drawings and presented in the form of a poster or magazine article.

Probleme und Konflikte

Page 45

1 Gehen sie gern zur Schule?

This reading task revises key vocabulary in preparation for **exercise 1** on **p.142** of the main course-book.

- Preparation: check comprehension of key vocabulary.
- Students decide which opinions about school are positive and which ones are negative.
- Check answers as a whole-class activity.
- Follow-up: students think up further positive and/or negative statements about school, using the sentences provided as models, but varying the adjectives used. Less able students create positive and negative wordsearches.

2 Wie findest du die Schule?

This listening task may be used as an introduction or easier alternative to **exercise 1a** on **p.156** of the main course-book. The recording is a simplified and shortened version of the material used with the main course-book.

- Students listen to the recordings and take brief notes about whether Andreas and Susanne like school and why not.
- Students then complete the two e-mails with the phrases from the box.
- Check answers as a whole-class activity.
- Students write out the e-mails in full, preferably using ICT.
- Follow-up: students adapt the e-mails to describe their own attitudes towards school.

Transcript

– Andreas, wie findest du die Schule? Gehst du gern zur Schule?
– Ja, ich gehe sehr gern zur Schule. Schule macht Spaß, finde ich.
– Warum gehst du gern zur Schule?
– Die Lehrer sind alle jung und total locker. Das gefällt mir gut. Sie sind auch sehr nett und sie sind überhaupt nicht autoritär. Das finde ich sehr wichtig.
– Und wie findest du den Unterricht?
– Auch super. Der Unterricht ist immer interessant – kein Fach ist langweilig.

– Und du, Susanne? Wie findest du die Schule? Gehst du gern zur Schule?
– Nein, ich gehe gar nicht gern zur Schule!
– Und warum gehst du nicht gern zur Schule?
– Also, der Unterricht ist viel zu trocken – total langweilig! Und meine Lehrer sind alle so streng – das ist furchtbar. Na ja, und dann die Hausaufgaben: Es gibt immer zu viele Hausaufgaben.
– Also, Schule macht keinen Spaß?
– Nein! Schule macht nur Stress, finde ich.

Page 46

3 Stress in der Schule

This matching task may be used as an introduction or easier alternative to **exercise 2** on **p.142** of the main course-book.

- Draw students' attention to the fact that there are two speech bubbles too many.
- Students match the speech bubbles to the pictures.
- Follow-up: students might like to draw cartoons to illustrate the two 'surplus' speech bubbles.

4 Du bist dran

This guided writing task is a more structured alternative to **exercise 5** on **p.143** of the main course-book.

- Preparation: draw students' attention to the *Hilfe* boxes on **pp.142–43** of the main course-book.
- Students write a letter or e-mail in response to Peter's questions.
- Follow-up: students conduct a survey of fellow students' views and record their findings.

TEIL 4

D Die Zukunft

Page 47

1 Was möchten sie später machen?

This matching task revises key vocabulary in preparation for **pp.148–49** of the main course-book.

- Preparation: revise *ich möchte/würde* + infinitive.
- Students match the speech bubbles to pictures.
- Follow-up: students list the sentences in their own order of preference.

Page 48

2 Pläne für die Zukunft

This task may be used as an introduction or easier alternative to **exercise 1** on **p.148** of the main course-book.

a This simple listening-for-gist task prepares students for task 1b below.

- Preparation: study the pictures with the class and elicit words to describe each one.
- Students listen to the recording in three sections and choose the picture which matches each speaker's aspirations.

b Students listen to the recording again for specific information.

- Preparation: remind students of the difference between statements which are false and those which are not mentioned in the text.
- Students listen to the recording and decide whether the statements are true, false or not in the text.
- Follow-up: students correct any statements containing errors.

Transcript

1 Ich bin der Pit und ich möchte mit 16 die Schule verlassen. Ich bin praktisch und arbeite gern im Freien. Also, ich würde gern eine Lehre machen – am liebsten eine Lehre als Gärtner.
2 Mein Name ist Kathi und ich würde gern Karriere machen! Das ist sehr wichtig für mich – ich möchte später viel Geld verdienen. Ich möchte deshalb nach dem Abitur eine Lehre als Bankkauffrau machen.
3 Ich heiße Rainer. Später würde ich gern heiraten und Familie haben – und ich passe dann auf die Kinder auf und mache den Haushalt und meine Frau geht arbeiten.

3 Was möchtest du später machen?

This oral pair-work task may be used as an introduction or more structured alternative to **exercise 3** on **p.149** of the main course-book.

- Preparation: go through the example dialogue with the whole class.
- Students work in pairs to create dialogues in response to the visual prompts, using the *Hilfe* box as necessary.
- Students go on to make up their own dialogues using the *Hilfe* box.
- Students can record their dialogues on tape or in writing.
- Follow-up: students conduct a class survey about plans for the future.

Page 49

4 Ein Jahr reisen?

This simple reading task may be used as an introduction or easier alternative to **exercise 4** on **p.149** of the main course-book.

- Preparation: revise the formation of the future tense.
- Students categorise the statements as 1 'go travelling for a year' or 2 'start work/studies straight away'.
- Check answers as a whole-class activity.
- Follow-up: students write further statements for their classmates to categorise.

5 Du bist dran

This speaking or writing task is a more structured alternative to **exercise 5** on **p.149** of the main course-book.

- Students use the diagram to construct sentences about their plans, using *weil*. The description can be spoken or written.
- More able students should be encouraged to adapt the model to express their own ideas.

Meine Arbeit

Page 50

1 Berufe, Berufe, Berufe …

This task revises basic jobs vocabulary in preparation for **pp.150–51** of the main course-book.

a Students complete column A of the grid with the job titles from the box.

b Students complete column B of the grid with the masculine or feminine equivalents of the job titles in column A.

- Follow-up: students extend the grid with other job titles they know.

Page 51

2 Was ist er/sie von Beruf?

This guided writing task may be used as consolidation of the structures used in **exercise 1** on **p.150** of the main course-book.

- Students write out the notes as full sentences.
- Follow-up: students embellish the notes with their own ideas.

Entscheidungen

1 Probleme und Konflikte

This matching task may be used as an introduction to **exercise 1** on **p.152** of the main course-book.

- Preparation: revise *ich möchte/muss* + infinitive.
- Students match the speech bubbles to the pictures.

2 Du bist dran

This writing task may be used as an introduction or easier alternative to **exercise 2b** on **p.153** of the main course-book.

- Preparation: brainstorm ideas for potential conflicts with the whole class. Assist students in putting their ideas into correct German.
- Students write three sentences describing conflicts in their lives. Point out that these need not be real: they can invent conflicts, or write as another person, e.g. a character in a soap opera.

E Wir suchen Stellen

Page 52

1 Bist du dafür geeignet?

This crossword consolidates work-related personality traits and may be used in conjunction with **exercise 1** on **p.154** of the main course-book.

- Preparation: draw students' attention to the *Hilfe* box on **p.154** of the main course-book, which contains all the adjectives which they need in order to complete the crossword.
- Students translate the adjectives into German and use them to complete the crossword.

2 Wie muss man sein?

This listening task may be used as an introduction or easier alternative to **exercise 2** on **p.154** of the main course-book.

- Students listen to the recording in five sections and note down the qualities required for each job.
- Check answers as a whole-class activity.
- Follow-up: students work in groups. One student suggests a profession; the student on his/her left or right has to suggest a suitable quality, and so on round the group.

Transcript

– Ich möchte Gärtnerin werden. Man muss kräftig sein. Man muss natürlich auch gern im Freien arbeiten!
– Ich möchte Lehrer werden. Ein guter Lehrer ist tolerant und auch geduldig.
– Ich möchte Ärztin werden. Man muss sehr sorgfältig sein. Man muss auch stark in Biologie sein.
– Ich möchte Mechaniker werden. Man muss praktisch sein und man muss sich auch für Technik interessieren.
– Ich möchte Verkäuferin werden. Ich bin dafür gut geeignet, weil ich höflich und kontaktfreudig bin.

Page 53

3 Wie und wo arbeitest du gern?

This matching task systematically consolidates expressions for talking about working conditions, and may be used in conjunction with **p.154** of the main course-book.

4 Interviewfragen

This matching task may be used as an introduction to **exercise 4** on **p.154** of the main course-book.

- Students match the questions to the answers.
- Follow-up: students work together in pairs to practise their own simple interviews, adapting the responses given.

TEIL 4

Page 54

5 Ein Lebenslauf

This guided writing task may be used as an alternative to **exercise 4b** on **p.154** of the main course-book.

- Students fill out the CV with their own details.

6 Sommerferienjobs

a This role-play task provides further practise of interview language and may be used in conjunction with **exercise 5** on **p.155** of the main course-book.

- Preparation: both students should look at the interview questions and jot down their own responses. They should refrain from writing out whole-sentence answers.
- Students play the roles of interviewer and interviewee for a job in a supermarket.
- The interview could be recorded on tape.

b This writing task is a follow-up to task 6a above and may be used as an alternative to **exercise 5b** on **p.155** of the main course-book.

- Preparation: draw student's attention to the letter on **p.155** of the main course-book, which they should use as a model for their own letter.
- Students write a letter of application for the job from task 6a, including as many as possible of the ideas which emerged from their role-play.

Ungesundes Leben

Page 55

1 Rauchen ist …

This reading task may be used as an introduction or easier alternative to **exercise 1a** on **p.156** of the main course-book.

- Students read the speech bubbles and categorise them as for or against smoking,
- Check answers as a whole-class activity and discuss any incorrect answers.

2 Was denken sie?

This writing task may be used as an introduction or easier alternative to **exercise 1b** on **p.156** of the main course-book.

- Students use the key words and the picture cues to construct sentences about attitudes towards smoking, drugs and alcohol.
- Check answers as a whole-class activity.
- Students write out a fair copy.
- Follow-up: students adapt the sentences, using other adjectives from **exercise 1a** on **p.156** of the main course-book.

Page 56

3 Warum?

This sequencing task revises the word order of subordinate clauses with *weil*. It may be used in preparation for **exercise 2** on **p.156** of the main course-book.

- Preparation: revise the word order of subordinate clauses.
- Students put the words in the correct sequence to form *weil* clauses.
- Check answers as a whole-class activity.
- Students write out a fair copy of the sentences.
- Follow-up: students write their own *weil* clauses, using those from the task as a model.

4 Du bist dran

This task may be used as an introduction or easier alternative to **exercises 2b** and **2c** on **pp.156–57** of the main course-book.

- Students note down their responses to the questions.
- Students record their responses on cassette. This could be done as pair-work, with one partner taking the role of interviewer and the other that of interviewee, before the roles are reversed.
- Follow-up: students conduct a class survey, or ask family and friends, and display the results as a magazine article or poster.

Leben und Probleme

1 Kreuzworträtsel

This crossword reinforces key vocabulary from **exercises 1** and **2** on **pp.158–59** of the main course-book.

- Preparation: point out to students that most of the words can be found in the text of **exercises 1** and **2** on **pp.158–59** of the main course-book.
- Students translate the English clues and complete the crossword.

TEIL 4

- Check the answers as a whole-class activity before students go on to task 2 below.

2 Das Leben ist nicht einfach!

This gap-fill task is a follow-up to task 1 above.

- Students use the words in the crossword to complete the sentences.

Kontrolle 1: Hören

Page 58

This section consists of two listening tests to measure students' understanding of a range of material covered in **Teil 4**.

1 Students listen to six teenagers describing themselves and write the appropriate number 1–6 in the box by each illustration a–f.

> **Transcript**
> 1 Ich bin immer schlecht gelaunt!
> 2 Ich bin sehr freundlich!
> 3 Ich bin sehr höflich – ich bin nie frech!
> 4 Ich bin immer gut gelaunt!
> 5 Meine Füße sind zu groß!
> 6 Hausaufgaben finde ich nicht gut – ich bin sehr faul!

2 Students listen to an interview with a teenage girl about her attitudes towards healthy living and the environment.

> **Transcript**
> – Hallo, Meike! Du, ich mache eine Umfrage für die Schule – über Gesundheit und die Umwelt. Machst du mit?
> – Ähm … ja, okay.
> – Also, zuerst ein paar Fragen zum Thema Gesundheit. Erste Frage: Wie kommst du zur Schule?
> – Ähm, ich fahre fast immer mit dem Bus.
> – Du fährst also nie mit dem Rad zur Schule?
> – Doch, manchmal fahre ich mit dem Rad. Aber meistens bin ich zu faul.
> – Und jetzt die zweite Frage: Wie viel Alkohol trinkst du?
> – Ach … sehr wenig! Ab und zu trinke ich am Wochenende ein Bier oder ein Glas Wein. Das ist alles.
> – Die dritte Frage: Rauchst du?
> – Tja, ich rauche so zehn Zigaretten am Tag. Ich weiß, das ist schlecht für die Gesundheit. Ich will damit aufhören, aber es ist nicht so einfach!
> – Und jetzt zum Thema Umwelt. Was tust du persönlich für die Umwelt?
> – Also, da muss ich nachdenken … Ja. Ich spare Energie.
> – Und wie machst du das?
> – Ich mache immer das Licht aus, wenn ich aus dem Zimmer gehe.
> – Gut. Ist das alles?
> – Nein – ich spare auch Wasser. Ich dusche immer, ich nehme nie ein Bad.
> – Und die letzte Frage: Ist deine Familie umweltfreundlich?
> – Also, meine Eltern sind sehr umweltfreundlich. Sie trennen immer den Müll und kaufen Pfandflaschen. Aber meine Schwester findet Umweltschutz nicht so wichtig. Sie kauft immer Getränke in Dosen, weil sie das bequemer findet. Und ihren Müll wirft sie einfach weg, ohne ihn zu trennen.

Kontrolle 2: Sprechen

Pages 59–60

This section is a list of suggestions for topics for oral presentations, taken from the topics covered in **Teil 4**.

Kontrolle 3: Lesen

Page 61

This section consists of two reading tests to measure students' understanding of a range of material covered in **Teil 4**.

1 Students match the pictures to the sentences.

2 Students read the letter and decide whether the statements are true, false or not in the text.

Kontrolle 4: Schreiben

Page 62

This section consists of three writing tests to measure students' understanding of a range of material covered in **Teil 4**.

1 Students write a letter of application for a holiday job in a bakery.

2 Students write an article about their school.

3 Students write a description of their town or village.

ANSWERS

Teil 1

Page 4
1a Auf Wiedersehen
1b 1 NAETZ – falsch: NEITZ; 2 MARTINA BAUM – richtig; 3 FIRINA – falsch: VERENA; 4 ANDREAS FRANC – falsch: ANDREAS FRANK; 5 FLOAEAN – falsch: FLORIAN
3 a 4; b 3; c 1; d 5; e 2

Page 5
1a 1 30; 2 95; 3 11; 4 17; 5 51; 6 78; 7 200; 8 60
1b 1 dreißig; 2 fünfundneunzig; 3 elf; 4 siebzehn; 5 einundfünfzig; 6 achtundsiebzig; 7 zweihundert; 8 sechzig
2a a 1; b 5; c 3; d 2; e 4
2c a Am sechsten November; b Am neunten Februar; c Am zwölften April; d Am einunddreißigsten Januar; e Am sechsundzwanzigsten Mai
3 1 b; 2 a; 3 b; 4 b; 5 c

Page 6
1 a 1, 3, 4, 6; b 2, 5, 7, 8
2a 1 lange; 2 eine; 3 Schnurrbart; 4 groß; 5 jung

Page 7
3a 1 ein Hund; 2 eine Katze; 3 ein Fisch; 4 ein Hamster; 5 eine Maus; 6 ein Kaninchen; 7 ein Wellensittich; 8 ein Meerschweinchen; 9 eine Schildkröte; 10 eine Kuh
4 a 1; b 4; c 2; d 3
5 1 einen, eine; 2 ein, eine; 3 einen, ein; 4 einen, einen; 5 ein, eine

Page 8
7

S	L	M	V	M	K	S	L	Z	H
T	E	A	E	E	E	E	E	A	J
A	H	N	R	K	L	K	H	H	A
M	F	N	K	N	L	T	R	N	H
B	A	E	Ä	O	N	Ä	E	Ä	R
L	F	S	U	R	E	P	R	R	Ü
K	A	U	F	F	R	A	U	Z	A
A	H	P	E	F	I	S	F	T	I
U	R	O	R	E	N	O	R	I	N
S	E	K	R	E	T	Ä	R	N	S
A	R	P	O	L	I	Z	I	S	T

8 1 Programmierer; 2 Lehrer; 3 Mechanikerin; 4 Kellnerin; 5 Polizist

Page 9
1 1 e; 2 a; 3 f; 4 b; 5 d; 6 g; 7 c
2 Ich heiße <u>Ernst</u> und ich bin siebzehn <u>Monate</u> alt. Ich habe <u>lange, lockige, schwarze</u> Haare und eine <u>Glatze</u>. Ich trage einen Ohrring und eine Sonnenbrille. Ich bin ziemlich groß und <u>sehr dick</u>. <u>Ich mag keine Tiere</u>. Ich habe vier <u>Kaninchen</u>.

Page 10
1 **Hanna:** Ich fotografiere gern. Ich schwimme gern. **Sabine:** Ich sammle Briefmarken. Ich lese gern. **Ralf:** ich spiele gern Fußball. Ich sehe gern fern. **Kalib:** Ich höre gern Musik. Ich spiele gern Klavier. **Jasmin:** Ich fahre gern Rad. Ich tanze gern. **Dieter:** Ich interessiere mich für Mode. Ich koche gern. **Helga:** Ich spiele gern Gitarre. Ich spiele gern Tennis.
2 1 ✔ dancing, music; ✘ football, reading
2 ✔ animals, stamps; ✘ music
3 ✔ football, dancing, music; ✘ stamps
4 ✔ reading; ✘ football, animals

Page 11
1 1 g; 2 d; 3 e; 4 b; 5 a; 6 c; 7 f

Page 12
1a 1 d; 2 c; 3 b; 4 e; 5 a
1c Ich bin auf einem tollen **Konzert**. Ich bin hier mit Tom (Mr Williams). Die Karten kosten **20 Euro**. Das Konzert ist **um 22.00 Uhr** zu Ende. Das Konzert ist super! Wir tanzen alle und es **gefällt** mir sehr gut. Später kaufe ich mir noch ein **T-Shirt** und **zwei Poster**. Am Ende **fahren** wir mit dem **Bus** zur Jugendherberge.

Page 13
1 1 V; 2 G; 3 V; 4 G; 5 V; 6 G; 7 G; 8 V; 9 V; 10 G
2 1 Ich habe Speck gegessen. 2 Er ist in die Disco gefahren. 3 Ich habe Kaffee getrunken. 4 Sie ist mit dem Auto gefahren. 5 Er hat ein T-Shirt gekauft. 6 Er ist zu Fuß gegangen. 7 Sie hat eine Bratwurst gegessen. 8 Ich habe Fußball gespielt.
3 1 habe; 2 ist; 3 hat; 4 bin; 5 hat; 6 hat; 7 ist; 8 hat

Page 14
4a 1 Ich bin aufgestanden. 2 Ich habe Frühstück gegessen. 3 Ich bin in die Stadt gegangen. 4 Ich habe im Park Fußball gespielt. 5 Ich bin nach Hause gegangen. 6 Ich habe einen Hamburger gegessen. 7 Ich habe ein Bad genommen. 8 Ich bin ins Bett gegangen.
4b *Suggested answers:* Ich bin um acht Uhr aufgestanden. Ich habe um acht Uhr dreißig

ANSWERS

Frühstück gegessen. Ich bin um neun Uhr in die Stadt gegangen. Ich habe um elf Uhr eine Pizza/zu Mittag gegessen. Ich bin um ein Uhr einkaufen gegangen. Ich bin um zwei Uhr nach Hause gegangen. Ich habe um vier Uhr Klavier gespielt. Ich habe um sechs Uhr Tennis gespielt. Ich habe um acht Uhr Abendessen gegessen. Ich bin um elf Uhr ins Bett gegangen.

Page 15
1   1 c; 2 g; 3 a; 4 e; 5 f; 6 b; 7 d
2   1 c; 2 d; 3 a; 4 f; 5 e; 6 b

Page 16
1a Aberdeen liegt in Schottland. Bangor liegt in Wales. Belfast liegt in Nordirland. Birmingham ist eine große Stadt in Mittelengland. Dublin ist in Irland. Newcastle-upon-Tyne liegt in Nordengland. Norwich liegt im Osten. Southampton ist eine mittelgroße Stadt im Süden.
2   a Ich wohne in einem Einfamilienhaus. b Ich wohne in einem Reihenhaus. c Ich wohne in einer Wohnung. d Ich wohne in der Stadtmitte. e Ich wohne an der Küste. f Ich wohne auf dem Land.

Page 17
1a a 8; b 6; c 11; d 9; e 5; f 12; g 7; h 3; i 10; j 4; k 2; l 1
2a 1 Falsch; 2 Richtig; 3 Falsch; 4 Falsch; 5 Richtig; 6 Falsch
2b 1 Christian wohnt in einem Reihenhaus. 3 Das Haus hat einen Garten. 4 Es gibt eine Garage. 6 Das Haus hat ein Wohnzimmer.

Page 18
3a a der Kleiderschrank; b der Computer; c das Bett; d der Spiegel; e das Poster; f das Kuscheltier; g der Schreibtisch; h die Kommode; i der Sessel; j die Lampe; k der Fernseher
4   a 3; b 5; c 2; d 1; e 4

Page 19
5   1 auf; 2 neben; 3 auf; 4 über; 5 an; 6 neben; 7 auf; 8 unter; 9 hinter; 10 vor

Page 20
1a a eine Eisbahn; b ein Theater; c ein Stadion; d ein Schwimmbad; e ein Kino; f ein Jugendklub; g eine Disco; h eine Kneipe; i ein Restaurant; j ein Sportzentrum
1b 1 theatre, restaurant; 2 theatre, leisure centre, restaurant, stadium; 3 theatre, leisure centre, youth club, stadium; 4 leisure centre, stadium

Page 21
1   1 e; 2 g; 3 b; 4 a; 5 d; 6 c; 7 f

2   a ✔; b ✘; c ✔; d ✘; e ✔; f ✔

Page 22
1   a 5; b 1; c 6; d 4; e 2; f 3
2   a 4; b 2; c 9; d 7; e 3; f 8; g 5; h 6; i 1
3   1 stehe; 2 wasche; 3 ziehe … an; 4 frühstücke; 5 gehe; 6 gehe; 7 mache; 8 esse; 9 sehe fern; 10 ziehe … aus; 11 nehme; 12 gehe

Page 23
1   1 d; 2 a; 3 g; 4 b; 5 f; 6 e; 7 c
3   a liest, lesen; b isst, essen; c sieht, sehen; d geht, gehen

Page 24
1   a Käse; b Honig; c Kaffee; d Pommes frites; e Hähnchen; f Nudeln; g Gemüse; h Jogurt; i Schinken; j Apfel

Page 25
3   *Suggested answers; minor variations in word order are possible.* 1 Ich trinke Tee zum Frühstück. 2 Ich esse ein belegtes Brötchen in der Pause. 3 Ich trinke Orangensaft oder Wasser zu Mittag. 4 Ich trinke Limonade oder Cola in der Pause. 5 Ich esse Brötchen mit Marmelade zum Frühstück. 6 Ich esse Fisch mit Salat zu Mittag.
4   a Ich esse gern Schokolade. Ich trinke gern Cola. b Ich esse nicht gern Jogurt. Ich trinke nicht gern Tee. c Ich esse nicht gern Würstchen, Nudeln und Äpfel. d Ich esse gern Pizza und Eis.
6   1 b; 2 d; 3 e; 4 c; 5 a

Page 26
1   1 Physik; 2 Erdkunde; 3 Geschichte; 4 Englisch; 5 Informatik; 6 Musik; 7 Biologie; 8 Sport; 9 Chemie; 10 Mathe; 11 Deutsch; 12 Kunst
2   Chemie ✔; Sport ✘; Französisch ✔; Mathe ✘; Informatik ✔; Geschichte ✘; Erdkunde ✔; Musik ✔; Physik ✔; Biologie ✘

Page 27
1   1 f; 2 d; 3 c; 4 b; 5 e; 6 a
2a Meine Schule heißt Franz-Gruber-Schule. Meine Schule ist **modern/groß**. Sie ist sehr **groß/modern** und liegt **auf** dem Land. Meine Schule ist eine **Gesamtschule**. Sie ist **gemischt**. Wir haben Jungen und **Mädchen**. Die meisten **Schüler** sind fleißig, aber einige sind **faul**. Die meisten Lehrer sind **freundlich**.
1   a Ich werde eine Prüfung machen. b Ich werde eine Klassenfahrt machen. c Ich werde im Chor singen. d Ich werde die Oberstufe besuchen. e Ich werde Sport machen.

Page 28
1   1 d; 2 b; 3 a; 4 c; 5 g; 6 e; 7 f

ANSWERS

2 Meine **Schule** heißt Gesamtschule Schiller. Sie ist ganz groß und sehr **modern**. Das Gebäude ist erst zwei Jahre alt! Das ist eine **gemischte** Schule und es gibt 1200 Schüler/innen. Wir tragen keine **Uniform**. Ich lerne **Deutsch**, Englisch, **Französisch**, Mathe, Naturwissenschaften und **Kunst** in der Schule. Meine Lieblingsfächer sind Chemie und **Biologie**, weil ich sie ganz **einfach** finde – mein **Traumberuf** ist Ärztin! Kunst mag ich auch sehr gern, aber **Mathe** finde ich sehr **schwierig** – das verstehe ich einfach nicht!

Page 29
1 **a** 2; **b**; 3; **c** 1
2 **a** ✗; **b** ✓; **c** ✓; **f** ✓; **h** ✗
3 **a** 4; **b** 2; **c** 5; **d** 1; **e** 3

Page 31
1 **Nachname:** Müller; **Vorname:** Dieter; **Alter:** 16; **Geburtstag:** 3. Mai; **Wohnort:** Köln; **Adresse:** Baumbergstraße 12; **Telefonnummer:** 32 70 46
2 **a** ✗; **b** ✓; **c** ✓; **d** ✗; **e** ✓; **f** ✗
3 **Jugendklub:** ja; **Disco:** nein; **Freizeitzentrum:** ja; **Lebensmittelgeschäft:** ja; **Post:** ja; **Grünanlagen:** ja; **Industrie:** nein

Page 32
1 Ich heiße Stephanie und mein Familienname ist Seeman. Ich bin **vierzehn** Jahre alt. Mein Geburtstag ist am **zwölften Mai**. Ich habe einen **Bruder**. Er hat **kurze, dunkle** Haare. Er heißt Jürgen und ist sehr freundlich. Ich habe auch eine **Schwester**. Sie heißt Inge und hat **lange, blonde** Haare und trägt eine **Brille**. Hast du **Geschwister**?
2 **a** Ich stehe auf. **b** Ich ziehe mich an. **c** Ich frühstücke. **d** Ich fahre (mit dem Rad) in die Stadtmitte. **e** Ich kaufe ein./Ich kaufe eine Hose. **f** Ich esse einen Hamburger. **g** Ich gehe ins Kino. **h** Ich fahre nach Hause. **i** Ich gehe ins Bett. **j** Ich lese.
3 **a** Ich bin aufgestanden. **b** Ich habe mich angezogen. **c** Ich habe gefrühstückt. **d** Ich bin (mit dem Rad) in die Stadtmitte gefahren. **e** Ich habe eingekauft./Ich habe eine Hose gekauft. **f** Ich habe einen Hamburger gegessen. **g** Ich bin ins Kino gegangen. **h** Ich bin nach Hause gefahren. **i** Ich bin ins Bett gegangen. **j** Ich habe gelesen.
4 *Students should mention the following features:* Sofa, Buch, Fernseher, Spiegel, Kommode, Poster, Bild, Lampe, Computer, Schreibtisch, Kuscheltiere, Kleiderschrank, Bett, Kuscheltiere. *Accept any sentences which are grammatically correct and supported by the picture.*

Teil 2

Page 34
1 **a** 2; **b** 5; **c** 1; **d** 3; **e** 8; **f** 7; **g** 6; **h** 4
2

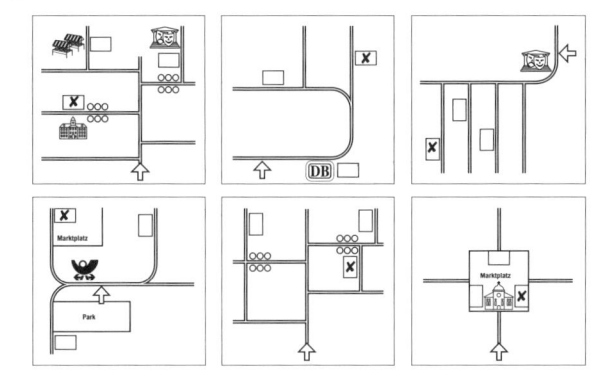

Page 36
1 **a** der Flughafen; **b** der Bahnhof; **c** der Reisebus; **d** die Fahrkarte; **e** die U-Bahn; **f** die Telefonzelle; **g** das Gleis; **h** die Autobahn; **i** die Haltestelle; **j** der Fahrplan
2 **a** Marktplatz; **b** Rathaus; **c** Theater; **d** Post; **e** Kino; **f** Bank; **g** Bahnhof; **h** Dom

Page 37
1a **Stadtmitte:** 10:15, 14:00, 17:45; **Waldeck:** 13:05, 16:50, 20:35
1b 1 Die Linie sechs. 2 Zwanzig Minuten. 3 Nein. 4 Am Markplatz. 5 11.30 Uhr
2 **a** 07:15; **b** 09:25; **c** 11:35; **d** 13:45; **e** 15:55; **f** 18:50

Page 38
3a **a** 6; **b** 3; **c** 2; **d** 4; **e** 5; **f** 1
3b **a** Um acht Uhr neun. **b** Um halb acht. **c** Um zwanzig nach zehn. **d** Um fünfundzwanzig vor neun. **e** Um Viertel nach neun. **f** Um halb neun.

Page 39
1 **a** 2; **b** 1; **c** 3; **d** 6; **e** 5; **f** 4
2a **a** 5; **b** 3; **c** 4; **d** 8; **e** 6; **f** 9; **g** 2; **h** 7; **i** 1
3a a, b, d, e, f, g

Page 40
4 Sehr geehrte **Damen** und Herren, ich besuche eine **Schule** in Oxford und bin in der zehnten **Klasse**. Wir möchten im **Juli** eine Klassenreise nach **Bonn** machen. Könnten Sie mir bitte eine **Broschüre** über die Stadt und eine **Liste** von Hotels zusenden? Ich hätte auch gern einen **Fahrplan/Stadtplan** und einen **Stadtplan/Fahrplan**. Mit freundlichen **Grüßen**

Page 41
1 1 e; 2 c; 3 g; 4 h; 5 d; 6 a; 7 b; 8 f

53

ANSWERS

Page 42
3a 1 e; 2 c; 3 b; 4 d; 5 a
3b 1 b; 2 d; 3 e; 4 a; 5 c

Page 43
4 1 Fähre gefahren; 2 (Reise)Bus gefahren; 3 Flugzeug geflogen; 4 Zug gefahren; 5 Auto gefahren
5a a 5; b 1; c 3; d 2; e 4
b 1 Pension; 2 Campingplatz; 3 Ferienapartment; 4 Jugendherberge; 5 Hotel

Page 44
1a a 4; b 2; c 6; d 5; e 3; f 1
2 **Haben Sie ein Zimmer frei?** – Have you got a room available? **mit Halbpension/Vollpension** – with half board/full board; **Für wie viele Nächte?** – For how many nights? **Was kostet das Zimmer?** – What does the room cost? **Ich habe ein Zimmer reserviert.** – I've reserved a room. **Gibt es einen Fernsehraum?** – Is there a TV room?

Page 45
3 1 Gasthof Wald oder Pension Alpenrose; 2 Hotel zur Sonne; 3 Hotel zur Sonne; 4 Gasthof Wald; 5 Gasthof Wald oder Pension Alpenrose; 6 Pension Alpenrose; 7 Gasthof Wald; 8 Pension Alpenrose
4 1 DORN, 1 Einzelzimmer, 3 Nächte, 1.8.–4.8.;
2 MEYER, 1 Doppelzimmer, 2 Nächte, 10.9.–12.9.;
3 SCHWARZ, 1 Einzelzimmer, 7 Nächte, 2.7.–9.7.;
4 KLEIN, 1 Doppelzimmer, 3 Nächte, 21.6.–24.6.

Page 46
5 B: Für wie viele Nächte? … Und für wann, bitte? … Ein Einzelzimmer oder ein Doppelzimmer? … Ja, das haben wir. … Mit Halbpension oder Vollpension? … Wie ist Ihr Name, bitte? … Gut, Herr Schmidt. In Ordnung.
6 1 meine Freunde und ich möchten drei Zimmer vom 12. bis zum 14. Juli reservieren. Wir möchten drei Einzelzimmer mit Dusche und WC. Wir hätten auch gern Vollpension.
2 meine Schwimmmannschaft und ich möchten fünfzehn Zimmer vom 16. bis zum 18. Mai reservieren. Wir möchten drei Doppelzimmer mit Bad und WC und zwölf Einzelzimmer mit Dusche und WC. Wir hätten auch gern Halbpension.
3 mein Jugendklub und ich möchten zweiundzwanzig Zimmer vom 9. bis zum 19. Juni reservieren. Wir möchten zwei Doppelzimmer mit Bad und WC und zwanzig Einzelzimmer mit Bad und WC. Wir hätten auch gern Halbpension.

Page 47
1 1 c; 2 d; 3 a; 4 b
2a a 4; b 2; c 1; d 3

Page 48
1 a 4; b 3; c 1; d 2
2a 1 21. März; 2 24. März; 3 drei; 4 zwei Mädchen; 5 ein Junge; 6 Frühstück und Mittagessen
3 a voll; b kaputt; c zu kalt; d geht nicht auf

Page 49
1 1 i; 2 h; 3 g; 4 e; 5 l; 6 j; 7 a; 8 d; 9 c; 10 b; 11 k; 12 f

Page 50
3 1 Wir haben eine Stadtrundfahrt gemacht. 2 Ich bin Ski gefahren. 3 Wir haben viele Souvenirs gekauft. 4 Ich bin im Meer geschwommen. 5 Wir haben in einem Ferienapartment gewohnt. 6 Ich bin zum Markt gegangen.
4 diesen Winter sind wir nach Österreich **gefahren**. Wir haben dort in einer kleinen Pension **gewohnt**. Morgens habe ich einen Skikurs **gemacht**. Nachmittags haben wir einen Ausflug in die Berge **gemacht**. Abends haben wir im Hotel **gegessen**. Danach sind wir ins Dorf **gegangen**. Meine Eltern haben ein Glas Wein **getrunken** – und ich habe in der Disco **getanzt**! Um 22 Uhr bin ich ins Bett **gegangen**.

Page 53
1 a Ich trinke gern Cola. b Ich esse gern Pommes frites mit Majonäse. c Ich esse gern Hamburger. d Ich trinke nicht gern Bier. e Ich esse nicht gern Bratwurst. f Ich esse nicht gern Hähnchen.
1 a die Gabel; b der Löffel; c das Messer; d das Salz; e der Pfeffer; f der Teller; g der Essig; h die Tasse

Page 54
1 1 d; 2 g; 3 h; 4 b; 5 k; 6 l; 7 i; 8 j; 9 c; 10 e; 11 f; 12 a
2 14 = vierzehn; 20 = zwanzig;
45 = fünfundvierzig; 62 = zweiundsechzig;
80 = achtzig; 99 = neunundneunzig;
100 = hundert; 200 = zweihundert;
500 = fünfhundert; 1000 = tausend
3 1 c; 2 e; 3 a; 4 b; 5 d

Page 55
4a 1 Schalter; 2 Briefmarke; 3 Luftpost; 4 Päckchen; 5 Brief; 6 Postkarte; 7 Briefkasten; 8 Kunde
4b a Postkarte; b Brief; c Briefmarke; d Luftpost; e Päckchen; f Kunde; g Schalter; h Briefkasten

ANSWERS

5 **a** Was kostet ein Brief nach England, bitte? **b** Was kostet eine Postkarte nach Frankreich, bitte? **c** Was kostet ein Päckchen nach Hamburg, bitte? **d** Ich möchte eine Briefmarke zu sechzig Cent, eine Briefmarke zu achtzig Cent und eine Briefmarke zu zwanzig Cent. **e** Ich möchte zwei Briefmarken zu sechzig Cent und drei Briefmarken zu zwanzig Cent. **f** Ich möchte drei Briefmarken zu einem Euro und eine Briefmarke zu sechzig Cent. **g** Ich möchte zwei Briefmarken zu einem Euro und fünf Briefmarken zu zwanzig Cent. **h** Ich möchte drei Briefmarken zu achtzig Cent und zwei Briefmarken zu sechzig Cent. **i** Ich möchte drei Briefmarken zu sechzig Cent und eine Briefmarke zu einem Euro.

Page 56
1 1 f; 2 d; 3 e; 4 c; 5 a; 6 b
2A 1 b; 2 c; 3 a; 4 a
2B 1 b; 2 a; 3 b
3 **a** Ulla; **b** Andreas

Page 57
a 1 Tabletten; 2 Hustensaft; 3 Augentropfen; **a** 1 Esslöffel vor dem Schlafengehen; **b** Alle 4 Stunden 1 Tropfen; **c** Dreimal täglich vor den Mahlzeiten
b 1 c; 2 a; 3 b

Page 58
1 **a** Ich habe meine Sonnenbrille verloren. **b** Ich habe meine Geldbörse verloren. **c** Ich habe meinen Rucksack verloren. **d** Ich habe meine Uhr verloren. **e** Ich habe meinen Schlüssel verloren. **f** Ich habe meinen Fotoapparat verloren. **g** Ich habe meine Tasche verloren. **h** Ich habe meinen Ring verloren. **i** Ich habe mein Armband verloren. **j** Ich habe meinen Schirm verloren.

Page 59
1 1 a; 2 b; 3 b
2 **a** 5; **b** 1; **c** 6; **d** 4; **e** 3; **f** 2; **g** 7; **h** 8

Page 61
1 1 a; 2 h; 3 g; 4 b; 5 f; 6 c; 7 i; 8 d; 9 e
2 1 Mit ihrer Familie; 2 Eine Woche; 3 Ein Einzelzimmer mit Fernseher und Balkon; 4 Bratwurst mit Pommes frites
3 1 R; 2 F; 3 N; 4 R; 5 N; 6 F; 7 F; 8 R

Page 62
1 1 Einzelzimmer; 2 Bad; 3 WC; 4 zehnten bis (zum) sechzehnten September; 5 einen Fernseher; 6 Halbpension.
2 *Suggested answer:* Sehr geehrte Damen und Herren, ich möchte ein Doppelzimmer mit WC und Dusche vom zweiten bis achten Mai reservieren. Ich hätte gern ein Telefon im Zimmer und Halbpension. Mit freundlichen Grüßen Sarah Williams
3 *Students should include the following information in their answers:* Ich mache zwei Wochen Urlaub in Österreich. Ich bin mit meinen Eltern hier. Wir sind mit dem Auto nach Österreich gefahren. Wir wohnen in einem Hotel. Die Sonne scheint jeden Tag.

Teil 3

Page 4
1 das Müsli, der Käse, das Brot, der Fisch, die Wurst, die Kartoffel, die Butter, das Fleisch, das Obst, der Apfelsaft, das Brötchen, die Marmelade, der Salat, die Schokolade, der Toast, das Gemüse, der Tee, der/das Jogurt, die Tomate, die Pommes frites

M	Ü	S	L	I	Y	G	A	B	J	C	P
A	X	C	K	Ä	S	E	B	R	O	T	O
R	S	H	T	F	I	M	J	E	G	O	M
M	A	O	O	D	N	Ü	O	K	U	M	M
E	L	K	A	F	I	S	C	H	R	A	E
L	A	O	S	G	H	E	M	L	T	T	S
A	T	L	T	W	U	R	S	T	Y	E	F
D	K	A	R	T	O	F	F	E	L	Q	R
E	P	D	R	B	U	T	T	E	R	W	I
F	L	E	I	S	C	H	V	O	B	S	T
A	P	F	E	L	S	A	F	T	Q	S	E
B	R	Ö	T	C	H	E	N	R	E	T	S

Page 5
3 1 hatte; 2 habe … gekocht; 3 bin … aufgestanden; 4 habe … gebacken; 5 habe … aufgeräumt; 6 habe … gedeckt; 7 bin … angekommen; 8 habe … gegessen

Page 6
1a 1 d; 2 g; 3 a; 4 i; 5 b; 6 e; 7 j; 8 h; 9 f; 10 c

Page 7
1a 1 c; 2 g; 3 e; 4 a; 5 d; 6 f; 7 b
2 1 Am 10. Oktober; 2 Bei Paul zu Hause; 3 Um acht Uhr; 4 Man hat getanzt, gegessen, getrunken; 5 Um Mitternacht; 6 Viel Spaß; 7 Nicht so toll, total langweilig

Page 8
1a 1 Obst; 2 Bananen; 3 Blumenkohl; 4 Orangensaft; 5 Salat; 6 Karotten
2a 1 Chips; 2 Schokolade; 3 Kuchen; 4 Marmelade; 5 Honig; 6 Kartoffeln

ANSWERS

3 **a** Ich esse am liebsten Hähnchen. **b** Ich esse nicht gern Kuchen. **c** Ich esse gern Süßigkeiten/Bonbons. **d** Ich esse gern Pommes (frites). **e** Ich esse am liebsten Gemüse. **f** Ich esse nicht gern Obst.

Page 9
1 **a** 6; **b** 4; **c** 3; **d** 5; **e** 2; **f** 1

Page 9
1 **Peter:** d, j; **Eva:** c, g; **Kai:** h, i; **Max:** f, b; **Fatima:** e, a
2 **Dafür:** 1, 5, 6, 8; **Dagegen:** 2, 3, 4, 7

Page 11
3a **Björn:** 4, 6, 7; **Golo:** 1, 3, 8; **Meike:** 2, 5, 9
3b **1** ✗; **2** ✓; **3** ✓; **4** ✗; **5** ✗; **6** ✗; **7** ✓; **8** ✗; **9** ✗

Page 12
1 **a** I; **b** K; **c** K; **d** I
2a **a** Ich arbeite als Verkäufer. **b** Ich arbeite als Krankenschwester. **c** Ich arbeite als Babysitter. **d** Ich arbeite an einer Tankstelle. **e** Ich arbeite als Zeitungsausträger./Ich trage Zeitungen aus. **f** Ich arbeite in einem Laden.

Page 13
3 Verkäufer, Samstag, 7 Stunden, 9 Euro; Zeitungsausträger, Mittwoch(nachmittag), 3 Stunden, 8 Euro
4a **1** a; **2** b; **3** c; **4** a; **5** c
4b *Possible answer:* Ich habe auch einen Job – ich arbeite jeden Sonntagnachmittag/jedes Wochenende als Kellner/in in einem Café. Die Arbeit ist anstrengend und ich bekomme nur 6 Euro pro Stunde. Das ist nicht viel Geld! Ich arbeite von 14 Uhr bis 18 Uhr.

Page 14
1a **1** c; **2** f; **3** e; **4** b; **5** d; **6** h; **7** a; **8** g

Page 15
2a ~~Jan Stade~~ Jens Staade, ~~60-30-21~~ 60 20 31, ~~Erdkunde~~ Englisch, ~~Englisch~~ Informatik, ~~nicht kontaktfreudig~~ sehr kontaktfreudig
3 **1** Richtig; **2** Falsch; **3** Nicht im Text; **4** Richtig; **5** Falsch; **6** Richtig; **7** Nicht im Text; **8** Richtig

Page 16
1 **a** langweilig; **b** interessant; **c** anstrengend; **d** aufregend; **e** stressig
2a **1** e; **2** h; **3** g; **4** d; **5** b; **6** a; **7** c; **8** f

Page 17
1 **1** Disco; **2** Schwimmen; **3** Stadt; **4** Theater; **5** Restaurant; **6** Tennis; **7** Fernsehen; **8** Kino

Page 18
3 **1** b, c; **2** a, c; **3** b, d; **4** a, c; **5** a, d; **6** a, d

Page 19
4a **a** 3; **b** 1; **c** 2

Page 20
5a **a** 5; **b** 1; **c** 8; **d** 4; **e** 2; **f** 7; **g** 6; **h** 9; **i** 3

Page 21
1a Nachrichten, Trickfilm, Seifenoper, Musiksendung, Gameshow, Natursendung, Film, Serie, Sportsendung, Talkshow

G	N	A	C	H	R	I	C	H	T	E	N	S	T
A	A	U	F	L	Q	O	J	Q	O	J	W	P	A
M	T	R	I	C	K	F	I	L	M	K	T	O	L
E	U	I	G	Z	W	P	K	W	P	S	Y	R	K
S	R	O	H	X	E	A	L	E	A	E	O	T	S
H	S	E	I	F	E	N	O	P	E	R	P	S	H
O	E	P	J	C	R	S	Z	R	S	I	D	E	O
W	N	A	K	V	T	D	X	T	D	E	F	N	W
E	D	S	F	B	Y	F	C	Y	F	L	H	D	K
M	U	S	I	K	S	E	N	D	U	N	G	U	X
T	N	D	L	N	U	G	V	U	G	Z	C	N	B
Y	G	F	M	M	I	H	B	I	H	X	B	G	M

1b news, cartoon, soap (opera), music show/programme, game show, nature programme/documentary, film, series, sport(s) programme, talk show/chat show

Page 22
1 **1** b; **2** d; **3** a; **4** e; **5** c
2 **Nele:** 60 Euro, Schulsachen, Klamotten, spart nicht
Felix: 20 Euro, Computerzeitschriften, Kino, spart 7 Euro
3 **1** b; **2** c; **3** a; **4** b

Page 23
4a *Suggested answers:* **Internetshopping:** zu Hause einkaufen, einsam, keine Menschen, praktisch, mit einer Kreditkarte bezahlen, (Sonderangebote); **Stadtmitte:** viel Stress, viel Lärm, viele Menschen, in die Stadt fahren, Sonderangebote, (mit einer Kreditkarte bezahlen)

Page 24
1 **1** Gramm; **2** Tafel; **3** Tüte; **4** Glas; **5** Schachtel; **6** Dose; **7** Flasche; **8** Kilo; **9** Becher
2 **1** Kilo; **2** Trauben; **3** Brötchen; **4** Gramm; **5** Tüte; **6** Mineralwasser; **7** Schachtel; **8** Schokolade
3 eine Flasche Mineralwasser, sechs Brötchen, ein Kilo Trauben, eine Tafel Schokolade, hundert Gramm Käse, zweihundert Gramm Wurst, ein Glas Marmelade, eine Tüte Chips

ANSWERS

Page 25

1a 1 Musikabteilung; 2 Geschenkartikel; 3 Bücher; 4 Zeitschriften; 5 Parfümerie; 6 Information; 7 Damenmode; 8 Kinderkleidung; 9 Elektrogeräte; 10 Computer-Shop; 11 Herrenmode; 12 Schreibwaren

1b **Bücher** 1 – K; **Computer** 1 – 2; **Kinderkleidung** K – 1; **Musik** E – K; **Schreibwaren** 1 – 2; **Zeitschriften** 2 – E

Page 26

2a

```
G  P  U  L  L  O  V  E  R  K
H  B  V  J  A  C  K  E  L  S
G  R  T  R  O  C  K  Q  H  K
T  U  R  N  S  C  H  U  H  E
W  H  E  M  D  Q  L  G  Y  F
T  R  L  J  E  A  N  S  C  Z
F  D  Y  S  K  L  E  I  D  X
F  K  B  L  U  S  E  H  P  A
```

2b Pullover c; Jacke h; Rock e; Turnschuhe b; Hemd g; Jeans f; Kleid a; Bluse d

3 **a** 3; **b** 4; **c** 2; **d** 1; **e** 6; **f** 5

Page 27

4 **Susi** Pullover; **Jan** T-shirt

5 1 i; 2 g; 3 h; 4 b; 5 c; 6 a; 7 e; 8 f; 9 d

Page 28

1 **a** A; **b** B; **c** B; **d** B; **e** A; **f** A
2 **a** 2; **b** 3; **c** 8; **d** 4; **e** 6; **f** 5; **g** 1; **h** 7
3 **Sven:** Kino, 20 Uhr; **Lena:** Café (Jugendzentrum), 18 Uhr; **Rainer:** zu Hause, 19.30 Uhr

Page 31

1 1 Musikabteilung; 2 Geschenkartikel; 3 Zeitschriften; 4 Schreibwaren; 5 Computer-Shop; 6 Bücher
2 **a** 1; **b** 3; **c** 4; **d** 6; **e** 5; **f** 2
3 1 auf eine Party; 2 mit Anke; 3 (vier Flaschen) Cola; 4 sehr gut; 5 zu Fuß; 6 seine Eltern

Teil 4

Page 34

1 **a** 3; **b** 6; **c** 2; **d** 1; **e** 7; **f** 8; **g** 5; **h** 4

3a Ich bin **sechzehn** Jahre alt und ich wohne in **Bremen**. Meine Hobbys sind **Sport/Lesen** und **Lesen/Sport**. **Humor** finde ich wichtig. **Pessimisten** finde ich nicht gut. Ich bin immer **lustig**, aber ich bin manchmal auch **ungeduldig**.

Page 35

1 **a** Philipp; **b** Uwe; **c** Kathi; **d** Annika; **e** Katja
2A 1 a; 2 c; 3 c; 4 a
2B 1 c; 2 b; 3 b; 4 a

Page 36

3 **Tina:** 5, 6; **Marie:** 2, 4; **Frieder:** 1, 3
4a 1 b; 2 c; 3 a
4b **a** 3; **b** 1; **c** 3

Page 37

1 1 oberflächlich; 2 treu; 3 gesellig; 4 lustig; 5 launisch; 6 geduldig; 7 pessimistisch; 8 locker; 9 ehrlich; 10 tolerant; 11 faul; 12 pünktlich

Page 38

2 Mein bester **Freund** heißt Matthias. Wir haben dieselben **Interessen**. Wir spielen im selben **Fußball**verein und gehen **zusammen** ins Kino oder in die Disco. Matthias ist ein Jahr älter als ich – er ist 16. Er ist **gesellig** und auch zuverlässig. Das einzige **Problem** mit Matthias ist, dass er manchmal ungeduldig ist. Das ist ein Problem, weil ich sehr **unpünktlich** bin! Er muss oft auf mich warten. Das **gefällt** ihm nicht, weil wir dann zu **spät** zum Fußballtraining kommen. Trotzdem **verstehen** wir uns sehr gut!

3 1 Falsch; 2 Richtig; 3 Falsch; 4 Nicht im Text; 5 Richtig; 6 Richtig; 7 Richtig; 8 Falsch

Page 39

1 1 c; 2 b; 3 b; 4 a; 5 c
2 1 Ich wohne in einem Einfamilienhaus am Stadtrand. 2 Wir haben sehr wenig Parks und Grünanlagen. 3 Der Verkehr ist schlimm und die Luft ist ungesund. 4 Ich kann hier nicht Rad fahren.

Page 40

1 **a** 4; **b** 2; **c** 3; **d** 1
2 **a** 4; **b** 2; **c** 1; **d** 3

Page 41

1a 1 f; 2 a; 3 e; 4 b; 5 g; 6 d; 7 h; 8 d
1b 1 ✔; 2 ✘; 3 ✘; 4 ✔; 5 ✘; 6 ✘; 7 ✔; 8 ✔

Page 42

2 *The 'eco-friendly' answers are:* 1 b; 2 a; 3 c; 4 b; 5 c

Page 43

1 1 e; 2 b; 3 c; 4 a; 5 f; 6 d
1 1 6; 2 mit 6 Jahren; 3 das Abitur; 4 alle; 5 Hauptschule; 6 alle Schüler/innen; 7 mit 15–16 Jahren; 8 fleißig; 9 Grundschule; 10 mit 16 Jahren

57

ANSWERS

Page 44
1a **positiv:** gut, bequem, modisch, schön, praktisch; **negativ:** altmodisch, unpraktisch, hässlich, unbequem, schlecht
2 1 werfen; 2 Hof; 3 darf; 4 bringen; 5 Fahrräder, abstellen; 6 Pausen, aufhalten

Page 45
1 **positiv:** 1, 4, 5, 8; **negativ:** 2, 3, 6, 7
2 **Andreas:** ... Ich gehe **sehr gern** zur Schule, weil Schule **Spaß macht**. Die Lehrer an meiner Schule sind **jung und locker**. Ich finde es auch gut, dass sie **gar nicht autoritär** sind. Der Unterricht ist super, weil alle Fächer **interessant** sind. ...
Susanne: ... Ich gehe **überhaupt nicht gern** zur Schule. Schule macht **nur Stress**! Die Lehrer an meiner Schule sind gar nicht locker – sie sind **sehr streng**. Der Unterricht ist trocken, alle Fächer sind **langweilig** und wir bekommen **zu viele Hausaufgaben**. Furchtbar! ...

Page 46
3 a 3; b 2; c 1; d 6; e 4

Page 47
1 a 4; b 2; c; 8; d 3; e 7; f 1; g 5; h 6; i 9

Page 48
2a a 2; b 3; c 1
2b 1 Falsch; 2 Richtig; 3 Nicht im Text; 4 Falsch; 5 Nicht im Text; 6 Richtig

Page 49
4 **Ein Jahr reisen:** 1, 4; **Gleich studieren/arbeiten:** 2, 3, 5, 6

Page 50
1a 1 Verkäuferin; 2 Feuerwehrmann; 3 Geschäftsfrau; 4 Büroarbeiter; 5 Informatikerin; 6 Mechaniker; 7 Tierärztin; 8 Kellner; 9 LKW-Fahrerin; 10 Arzt

Page 51
2 *Suggested answers:* 1 Ich heiße Max Weber. Ich bin Büroarbeiter in Hamburg. Ich arbeite von 8 Uhr bis 18 Uhr. Ich finde meine Arbeit toll.
2 Ich heiße Helga Meyer. Ich bin Polizistin in der Stadtmitte. Ich arbeite von 10 Uhr bis 19 Uhr. Ich finde meine Arbeit anstrengend.
3 Ich heiße Pamela Schreiber. Ich bin Kellnerin im Hotel König. Ich arbeite von 17 Uhr bis 23 Uhr. Ich finde meine Arbeit interessant.
4 Ich heiße Ernst Erdmann. Ich bin Informatiker in Leipzig. Ich arbeite von 7 Uhr bis 17 Uhr. Ich finde meine Arbeit stressig.
1 a 1, 5; b 2, 6; c 3, 4

Page 52
1 1 tolerant; 2 sorgfältig; 3 locker; 4 kontaktfreudig; 5 geduldig; 6 kräftig; 7 praktisch; 8 höflich
2 1 kräftig, gern im Freien arbeiten; 2 tolerant, geduldig; 3 sorgfältig, stark in Biologie; 4 praktisch, sich für Technik interessieren; 5 höflich, kontaktfreudig

Page 53
3 a 7; b 2; c 6; d 5; e 1; f 4; g 3
4 1 c; 2 d; 3 b; 4 e; 5 a

Page 55
1 1 F; 2 G; 3 F; 4 F; 5 G; 6 G; 7 F; 8 G
2 1 Hannes findet Rauchen cool. Er findet Alkohol erwachsen. 2 Astrid findet Alkohol toll. Sie findet Drogen ekelhaft. 3 Monika findet Rauchen teuer. Sie findet Drogen ungesund. 4 Mehmet findet Drogen gefährlich. Er findet Rauchen ungesund.

Page 56
3 1 weil es so ungesund ist; 2 weil alle meine Freunde das machen; 3 weil ich sie gefährlich finde; 4 weil das cool aussieht; 5 weil ich dazu keine Lust habe

Page 57
1 **Waagerecht:** 1 träumen; 4 geschieden; 5 bezahlen; 7 Anfang; 8 Wohnung; 9 einsam; **Senkrecht:** 2 umgezogen; 3 verdienen; 6 Leben; 7 arbeitslos
2 1 umgezogen; 2 Leben; 3 Anfang; 4 einsam; 5 arbeitslos; 6 bezahlen; 7 geschieden; 8 Wohnung; 9 verdienen; 10 träumen

Page 58
1 a 4; b 1; c 6; d 2; e 3; f 5
2 1 b; 2 a; 3 b; 4 c; 5 c; 6 a

Page 61
1 1 e; 2 a; 3 f; 4 b; 5 d; 6 c
2 1 Falsch; 2 Falsch; 3 Richtig; 4 Falsch; 5 Nicht im Text; 6 Falsch